# THE STORY OF AFRICA

from the earliest times

Book Two

A. J. Wills

## HODDER AND STOUGHTON

LONDON SYDNEY AUCKLAND TORONTO

The day of Africa is yet to come

DAVID LIVINGSTONE

ISBN 0 340 0944 0

First published 1969
Fourth impression 1976

Copyright © 1969 A. J. Wills
Line drawing copyright © 1969 Hodder and Stoughton Ltd

Represented in West Africa by
C. M. Kershaw, M.A., P.O. Box 62, Ibadan, Nigeria
Represented in East and Central Africa by
K. W. Martin, P.O. Box 30583, Nairobi, Kenya

Printed in Great Britain for
Hodder and Stoughton Educational,
a division of Hodder and Stoughton Ltd, London,
by Butler and Tanner Ltd, Frome and London

# Preface

The aim of this two-year course, of which this volume is the second part, is to provide an overall history of Africa for junior secondary schools. The continent and its peoples are treated as a whole, and their story is set in the perspective of world developments since ancient and classical times. It is hoped that such a course will provide the basis of a more detailed regional study later. In learning about the origin and history of peoples in other regions of the continent, African children can gain a better understanding of how their own background fits into the whole.

The first book, after describing the origins of man in Africa, the influence of the early civilizations, and the great migrations of the Iron Age, concluded with the early medieval history of East Africa, both inland and on the coast.

This second-year book deals first with Islam in North Africa, and then with the West African empires and the forest kingdoms, including the medieval period. An account of the arrival of Portuguese and other traders from overseas both on the west and the east coasts is followed by chapters on the interior of east and south-east Africa from the sixteenth to the nineteenth centuries. The book concludes by returning to the West African scene in the nineteenth century. No attempt is made to relate the exploits of European explorers, or to deal with the partition and colonization of Africa which followed, but a final chapter discusses the main influences upon African history as far as the present day.

It is expected that the teacher will have access to regional histories in the school library from which he can obtain more detailed knowledge for story-telling and explanation of the characters and events related only briefly here. Some questions suggested for the guidance of the teacher are included at the end.

A. J. W.

# Contents

# Acknowledgments

The author and publisher are grateful to the following for permission to reproduce the photographs on the pages indicated:

Aerofilms Ltd   65, 92, 105
Mike Andrews   96
Barnaby's Picture Library   91
Trustees of the British Museum   13 (right), 31, 46, 50 (both), 72 (bottom)
British Museum Natural History   36
Camera Press Ltd   19, 42, 48
J. Allan Cash   109
Crown Copyright   67
Mary Evans Picture Library   9, 28, 107 (both)
Mansell Collection   7, 26, 63, 72 (top), 74, 104, 112, 116, 120 (left), 123
Popperfoto Ltd   10, 12, 13 (left), 14, 15, 16, 17, 27, 44, 56, 58, 66, 71, 78, 90, 101, 103, 113, 114 (both), 117, 120 (right), 121, 126
Portuguese State Office   55
Radio Times Hulton Picture Library   11, 64, 122, 124, 129
Tanzanian Information Services   82, 87, 88

The illustration on page 51 is taken from the book of a Dutch geographer, Olphert Dapper (1668)

The extracts on pages 23, 70 and 133 are taken from *The African Past* by Basil Davidson. They are reproduced by permission of Longmans, Green and Co. Ltd

# 1 Islam in the north and west

In the last chapter of Book One we read how Arabs came to live on the east coast of Africa, and how this was partly due to the growth of the faith of Islam in Arab countries.

Islam had an even greater effect on North and West Africa. In this chapter we shall see how the new religion began, and some of the far-reaching developments that followed.

**Islam**

The Arabs in Arabia, until the sixth century, were divided into different tribes and worshipped many different gods. The most important god, however, respected by all, was believed to be a black meteorite stone that was kept in the temple at Mecca. Many people from all over Arabia used to come and kiss the stone, and the merchants of Mecca grew rich on their custom.

Mohammed, a Meccan camel-driver born in 570, made journeys as far as Palestine and met many people including Jews and Christians. He became convinced that there were not many

*Early drawing of the Great Mosque at Mecca*

gods, but only one God. When he began to preach in Mecca, however, the leaders of the city grew jealous and an attempt was made to take his life. Mohammed's escape, called the *Hijra*, from Mecca to Medina in 622 is taken as the starting point of the new religion.

This new faith, called *Islam*, which means 'submission' (to the will of God), condemned idolatry and taught all Moslems to treat one another as brothers, to be considerate to their families and to obey the rules of prayer. They must convert the world, by force if need be. Mohammed, indeed, declared a *jihad* or 'holy war'. The new faith began to spread like wildfire among the Arab tribes.

## The first conquests of Islam

After Mohammed died in 632, his followers were inspired with his vision. The Arab tribes of the Yemen were united in an exultant resolve to spread the word of the Prophet through Arabia and beyond. To die in such a 'holy war' was to pass straight to Paradise. United under Mohammed's friend, Abu Bekr, who called himself the Khalif or 'Successor', the Arabs found that not even the hired armies of Byzantium could withstand the speed and ferocity of their northward advance.

Within four years of the Prophet's death, Syria was overrun. Soon Mesopotamia and Persia fell to Arab arms. Meanwhile a great Arab soldier, Amr-ibn-al-As, fell upon the rich fields of Egypt. By 642 the Arabs were rulers of the Lower Nile valley and Alexandria. A new phase in African history had begun.

Then the Arabs turned south, towards the Upper Nile. Here lived the Nubians, that fiercely independent people who had resisted the Romans, troubled the kingdom of Meroe, and fought with the armies of Aksum. These Nubians were the first people to check the all-conquering Arabs. They were skilful bowmen, and were as accustomed to desert fighting as the Arabs themselves. Moreover, following the example of the Aksumites two hundred years earlier, the Nubians had become Christians. They had been converted by missionaries from Egypt and Syria in about 550. Strengthened by a faith as inspiring as that of Islam itself, they resisted all Arab attempts at conquest.

In 652 the Arabs made a treaty with the Nubians. It was agreed that as long as Nubia continued to send gold and slaves down the Nile, as they had always done, the Arabs would leave their country alone. This treaty lasted for six hundred years.

*The Sahara Desert*

**Al Mahgrib**

Next the Arabs turned to the west, and soon conquered Libya as far as Cyrenaica.

Beyond Libya, they faced five hundred miles of waterless desert. This desert separated them from the fertile lowlands that stretch from Tunis to Morocco between the Atlas Mountains and the sea. This stretch of desert coast was to affect the whole future history of North and West Africa, because the Arabs in Egypt were never able properly to control the lands beyond it.

These lands, the fertile coastlands of the Atlas region, were called by the Arabs *Al Mahgrib*, which means 'The West'. Three centuries before, they had been rich provinces of the Roman Empire. Vandal raiders from Spain, as we have seen, had driven the Romans out and destroyed their cities. Now the country was inhabited by the original Berber population. They had mostly lost the Christianity of Roman times.

The Arabs now crossed the desert coast, and in 705, after thirty years of hard fighting, they were in control of Ifriq'iya (the old Roman province of 'Africa') and had founded a new capital at Tunis. They went on to occupy Numidia and Mauretania. Most of the Berbers were quickly converted to the new faith. In 711 an Arab army crossed the Straits of Gibraltar and invaded Spain.

## Divisions in Islam

While these conquests were being made, a dispute about the leadership of Islam occurred.

The leader of Islam was known as the Khalif. The first Khalifs after the death of Mohammed were men, like Abu Bekr, who had known the Prophet. However, when the third Khalif, Othman, was assassinated in 655, the Arabs disagreed about who should be their next leader. Most of them decided

*Mosque in Damascus, Syria*

*A gateway in Baghdad*

to follow Mu'awiya, the governor of Damascus, who spoke Greek. Mu'awiya declared that his son would succeed him, thus founding a new dynasty which was called 'Umayyad'.

Many Moslems, however, did not like this new dynasty, and new groups were formed, some of whom, as we read in the last chapter, went to live in East Africa. This disagreement was important, because any Moslems who were faithful to Islam but also wanted to break free from the Arab Empire could say they belonged to a group which disagreed with the Umayyads.

Ninety years later, in 749, there was another quarrel among the Moslem leaders. The Umayyads were removed, and a new dynasty, called the Abbasids after their founder, Abdul Abbas, occupied the Khalifate.

The Abbasids made an important change. Until this time, the capital of the Arab Empire had been at Damascus in Syria, although Mecca in Arabia was always the religious centre of Islam. Now the Abbasids founded a new capital at Baghdad on the River Euphrates. Baghdad was a rich city, but it was much farther east. This helped the Moslems to make conquests in Afghanistan and northern India. However, it made it more difficult to hold together the vast Arab Empire in the west.

## The isolation of the Mahgrib

In this way, the western part of North Africa, Al Mahgrib, became separated from the main Arab Empire for four reasons.

Firstly, five hundred miles of desert lay beyond Libya. Secondly, the Berber inhabitants were an independent-minded people who did not like to be ruled by Arabs. Thirdly, these inhabitants took advantage of the religious divisions of Islam to break away from the Khalifate. Fourthly, the new capital at Baghdad was too far away for effective control.

As a result, semi-independent Moslem states were formed in Ifriq'iya (Tunis), in Tahert in the central Mahgrib, in Morocco and in Spain. In this part of Africa the Berber people were all converted to Islam, and the Christianity that had existed there from Roman times was finally extinguished.

This was not so in Egypt. When the Arabs had conquered Egypt in 641, they had made an agreement with the Egyptian Christians that they could keep their own religion. This Egyptian or 'Coptic' church was to flourish in the centuries ahead, and even kept in touch with the Christians of the far-off highlands of Ethiopia, and of Nubia in the eastern Sudan.

*Coptic Church near Tura, Egypt*

*Ethiopian Coptic cross*

*Ethiopian drawing of a saint: 17th century*

## Links with West Africa

Now you will remember that the Berber peoples of North Africa were linked with the Negro peoples of the Sudan by trade routes which crossed the Sahara. Arab religion and culture now spread along these routes. Arabs did not spread the faith of Islam by war alone. Once the Arab empires had been established, the work of converting was carried on by missionaries and traders.

Arabs from the east looked upon the Mahgrib, and even farther-off places like Spain in the north-west and the Sudan in the south-west, as colonies to be settled in. In the same way

*Damascus: the burial ground where two of the wives of the Prophet and his daughter Fatima are interred*

as they had colonized the east coast, Arabs came to settle in the west among the Spaniards, the Berbers and the Negroes. Arabic became the language of religion and of trade. Trade, just as much as conquest, brought the religion of Islam and the education of Arab civilization across the Sahara from the Mahgrib to the Sudan.

Before we come to events in the Sudan, however, we must follow their course in the Mahgrib a little further.

**An empire in the Mahgrib**

The Berbers in the Mahgrib had been converted to Islam, but neither they nor the Arab colonists liked to think that they were the subjects of the far-off Khalifate in Baghdad. They liked it less because that Khalifate was becoming more Persian and less Arab all the time.

About 900, therefore, a Berber tribe called Kutama started

a revolt. They did so in the name of a separate branch of Islam, which believed that the Abbasid Khalifs had no right to rule. Instead, the Berbers produced their own leader, who claimed to be the true descendant of Fatima, the wife of the Prophet.

Before long, these Fatimids were using the title of Khalif. They aimed to conquer the whole of Islam. Soon they were attacking Egypt, which fell in 969. Four years later a new capital on the Nile was built for the Fatimid Khalif Al Mu'izz. This capital was called Al Kahira, for which the modern name is Cairo.

The Fatimids were able to conquer Syria, but they went no farther than this. Before long, they were driven back by the Turks, who had arrived from the east and become Moslem. The Turks were powerful fighters, and in 1171 their great leader, Al Saladin, drove the Fatimids out of Egypt.

Meanwhile, the Berbers in the Mahgrib had already thrown off their allegiance to Cairo. The Fatimid Empire was at an end.

*Damascus: the tomb of Saladin*

## The Almoravids

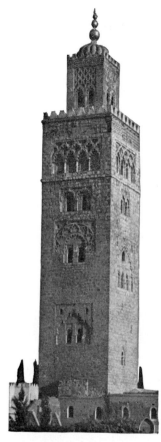

*The great minaret of the Kulubiya Mosque at Marrakesh, built by the Almohads in the 12th century*

Already, however, a new leader had appeared in the west. This happened among the Berber tribe of the Sahara region called Tuareg. The Tuareg were a fierce, hard-living people, whose menfolk wore the veiled head-dress which has made them famous.

In the eleventh century (about 1050), a Tuareg chief made the long pilgrimage to Mecca. Arrived there, he found that the true worship of Islam was a finer thing than the Berbers knew. Their own religious life had become slack. Determined to re-form Islam in his country, he brought back with him an Arab teacher whose name was Ibn Yasin.

Ibn Yasin was not liked by the Tuareg. His rules for living were too strict. They burnt his dwelling and drove him away. However, Ibn Yasin was not daunted. With two companions, he went to a remote place and stayed in retreat for several months, preparing to lead a religious revival.

Such a place of retreat, or hermitage, is called in Arabic *ribat*, and Ibn Yasin's followers came to be called the Al Mura-bitin, or Almoravids. We do not know where the *ribat* was. Some say that it was an island in the Senegal River; others that

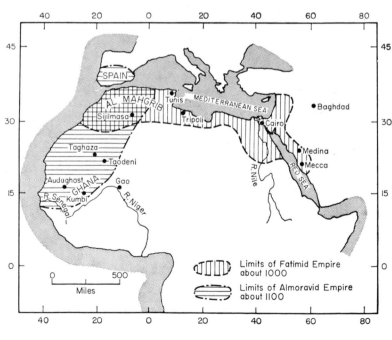

*Islam in North Africa*
*1000–1100*

it was an island in the sea, off the coast of Morocco.

His plans made, Ibn Yasin returned to the Mahgrib. Now his ideas spread like wildfire among the northern desert tribes. Men flocked to his banner. King Yahia of the Tuareg saw the opportunity to build an Almoravid empire. He decided to capture the whole Taodeni trail. In 1054 he took Audaghost at the southern end. Audaghost, in fact, was the northern outpost of Ghana. Two years later King Yahia marched north into Morocco. In 1057 he was killed in battle.

The next twenty years brought success to the Almoravids. They were now led by a great statesman, Abu Bekr. In the north, first Morocco and then Spain were conquered. In the south, Abu Bekr made an alliance with the Fulani, and conquered Ghana. Kumbi Saleh, their capital city, was captured in 1076. We shall hear more of this in the next chapter.

## The end of the Berber Empires

*A Tuareg tribesman*

The empire of the Almoravids did not last. When they became powerful over so large an area, their energy and the purity of their religion began to disappear. The Moroccan tribes of the Atlas Mountains did not like the Tuareg of the desert, and about 1125 they produced their own religious leader, Ibn Tumart. His followers, called Almohads—'people who say there is one God'—soon overran Morocco and Spain, and by 1159 they were rulers of the whole of the Mahgrib.

The Almohads were capable rulers, and made towns like Marrakesh and Fez into beautiful cities. But they were not able to impose unity on the Berber tribes for long. After a hundred years (by 1250), the Mahgrib had broken up again into its tribal parts. Finally there were the three countries that we know today as Tunisia, Algeria and Morocco.

The Negro peoples of the Sudan formed no part of these Berber states. Once more the connecting link was reduced to the age-old trans-Saharan trade routes.

However, for a short time in the eleventh century, the Almoravid 'explosion' had brought the Negroes into touch with Berber government and, what is more important, the religion of Islam. In the twenty years from 1070 to 1090, Islam came to the Negro states of Ghana on the Upper Niger, of Songhai at Gao, and of Kanem north of Lake Chad. The Hausa alone resisted the new faith for a time. In the next chapters we follow the stories of these Negro states.

## 2 Old Ghana

The old kingdom of Ghana was quite different from the Ghana of today. It was in a different place, north of the Niger, and inhabited by different people. There are links between the two, as we shall see, which is why the present state of Ghana was given its name; but these links are frail.

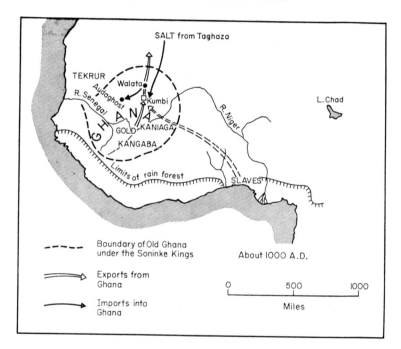

*The kingdom of Old Ghana*

**How Ghana began**

One of the oldest trans-Saharan trails crossed the desert from Morocco to the Middle and Upper Niger. This was the Taodeni trail. It had three advantages. It was shorter than the others because the Niger, flowing north into the desert, meets its southern end. The Sahara could be crossed in six weeks by the Taodeni. Secondly, it avoided the harsh terrain and brigand-infested ravines of the Hoggar Mountains. Finally, it linked the rich, salt-bearing ground south of the Moroccan Atlas with the gold of the Upper Niger region.

Salt and gold, in this part of Africa, were the great objects of trade from ancient times. Compared with them slaves and,

*Berber riding camel*

## Berber kings in Ghana

later, cloth were less important. Gold had been eagerly sought in Europe since Roman times. Europe had little gold, and the treasures of Egypt were used up. Some gold was found in the east, most of it coming from the Sudan. From the early Middle Ages, West African gold gleamed on the crowns and in the coffers of the popes and kings of Christendom.

Out of this trade were born the Negro states of the Sudan. The Mandingo in particular lived across the trade route between the salt supplies of the desert and the gold resources of the Senegal-Niger watershed.

During the first few centuries A.D., in the time of the Roman Empire, the Mandingo were simple farmers and herdsmen. They lived in small villages of simple huts and most of their tools were of stone. They allowed Berber traders to pass through their country in peace. They watched them and learned from them, so that in time they began to take part in the trade themselves. The Mandingo bought gold from the forest tribes to the south, and traded it with travellers from the north. From these Berber travellers they bought salt and other goods.

Now some of the Mandingo communities began to grow richer. One of them, in late Roman times, became the kingdom of Ghana. Though a small chiefdom at first, its ruler could afford to pay and equip soldiers, and so have order in the kingdom and power over neighbours. Traders could be compelled to pay taxes. In such a way, all the nations of the world have built up their power.

About the end of the Roman period, perhaps in the fifth century, the camel was introduced into North Africa from Arabia. This made a great difference. The desert was drying up and horses could no longer survive the hot, thirsty journey. Now, with the camel, trade increased again. More Berber traders came, their camel caravans laden with goods. When the Romans were driven from North Africa, the Berbers were free to develop the trade themselves.

Because of their wealth and their camel transport, some Berber traders were able to become powerful in Mandingo country, just as, in recent times, Arab traders were able to make themselves chiefs in East Africa. In this way, they could organize the trade more to their own profit. Instead of paying taxes, they received taxes themselves.

In this way, the Mandingo state of Ghana was ruled by Berber trader chiefs for over four hundred years. Mandingo traditions say that they had 'white' or Berber rulers from about 400 to about 630. Then came a change of dynasty, and a new line of Berber kings ruled until about 850.

Of the history of Ghana during this time we know little. Probably the most important development was the increasing use of iron for all kinds of implements and weapons. The gold trade also continued to grow. Towards the end of the Berber period, in 730, an Arab astronomer and geographer, Al Fazari, put the kingdom of Ghana on a map, and wrote of it simply as 'the land of gold'.

In civilization, however, Ghana was still backward. The chief's capital town was still built of mud houses. The art of writing was not known among the people, and there were no schools. Travellers brought news of the great Prophet and his teaching, but few were converted and the old pagan beliefs were still supreme.

## The Soninke kings

About 850, a revolution took place in Ghana. The people of the country rose up against their rulers and put a Negro dynasty, of the Soninke clan, upon the throne. The Berber king was killed, but there is no story to say why. Probably the Moslem conquest of the Mahgrib had upset the Berber states north of the Sahara. This might have reduced trade across the desert for a time, and weakened Berber control of the Sudan.

Many Berbers from Ghana fled west to Tekrur. We believe that there, by mixing with the Negro Tucolor and Wolof tribes, they formed the Fulani people.

The Soninke kings ruled Ghana for two hundred years. It was a time of growing prosperity. Trade revived, and then the Negro people themselves reaped all the benefit. Towns grew larger, and the ruler now lived in a fixed capital called Al Ghaba. Though the Soninke were still pagans, so many Moslems now traded in the country that the separate town of Kumbi Saleh was built for them a few miles from Al Ghaba itself. The Ghana Empire was extended to the Senegal River in the west and to the great bend of the Niger in the east. Its southern boundary was in the hills of the watershed, while to the north the frontier town of Audaghost looked out across scrub country of the desert fringe.

The fame of Ghana spread to far away Arabia. Arab travellers made the long journey to see the country. About 970 one of them, Ibn Hawqal, reported that the Emperor of Ghana was 'the richest in the world because of his gold'. At the end of the Soninke period a great geographer, Al Bekri, described the gold ornaments on the uniforms and weapons of servants and guards at the royal court at Al Ghaba. The Emperor's horse was tethered to a gold nugget weighing thirty pounds. His robes were of oriental silk. Great honour was done him at his court. In his army of 200,000 men, 40,000 were bowmen. The palace was built of stone, and twelve stone mosques stood in the neighbouring Moslem town of Kumbi Saleh.

Most of the people were still pagan, but Moslems, because they could read and write, held important posts in the government. These Moslems were Negroes. Berber traders came and went, but they had no power.

However, this was suddenly to change. Out of the north came the whirlwind of a new Berber conquest.

## The Almoravids

In the last chapter we read how the Almoravid religious revival sprang up in the Mahgrib. In 1065 Ibn Yasin himself led an army to the frontier town of Audaghost and, wrote El Bekri, 'took it by storm, carrying off all they found there'. Fifteen years later, in 1069, Abu Bekr declared a *jihad* or 'holy war' against Ghana, and a Berber army swept across the desert. In 1076 Kumbi was taken and sacked, and the Soninke Empire was no more.

This time, Berber rule in Ghana did not last for long. The Almoravids, as we shall see, were to be driven out by a new Negro uprising after only seventy years. But these seventy years were to have deep and lasting effects on the history of West Africa.

First of these effects was the spread of Islam. The Soninke kings had been pagan. The new rulers were Moslems, and many of the people were persuaded to follow the Prophet. The new faith spread, not only in Ghana, but down the Niger for a thousand miles. We must not suppose that all the people became converted in a short time, but by 1100 Islam was the strongest religion throughout the Negro peoples of the western Sudan. With it came the birth of education and learning.

The second effect of the Almoravid conquest was the movement of peoples. Some tribes, rather than accept the new faith, and fearing the onslaught of the Almoravid armies, fled south-east from Ghana across the Niger. It is possible that the ancestors of the Akan people of modern Ghana were among these groups who moved south from old Ghana to escape the *jihad*. Others, however, say that the Akan came from the north.

Lastly, the Empire of Ghana never recovered from the conquest.

## The decline of Ghana

The fact is that the peoples of Ghana had never been strongly united. Even under the Soninke kings there had been quarrels. The Mandingo were divided between the Soninke clan in the north and the Walinke in the south. Both had disputes with subject Berber tribes such as the Lemta of Audaghost. Soon after the conquest, these quarrels broke out again.

Two rival groups opposed each other in Central Ghana. West of Kumbi were the Sosso, whose king Sumanguru plundered Kumbi itself in 1203. But the Sosso feared the kingdom of Kangaba in the south. When the chief of Kangaba died, Sumanguru tried to kill all the chief's twelve sons so that none should succeed him. Eleven of them were indeed put to death, but the twelfth was a sickly child, and the soldiers spared his life. His name was Sundiata.

For twenty-five years till his death in 1235, Sumanguru was the strongest chief in Ghana, but his rule was not complete and the empire continued to crumble. Indeed, Ghana was no longer an empire at all by 1240, when Sundiata, who had been living in exile farther down the Niger, arrived at the head of an army and defeated the Sosso on the decisive field of Krina.

There is much to be told of Sundiata, but it belongs to the story of Mali, of whose empire he was the founder king.

The King of Ghana can put two hundred thousand warriors in the field, more than forty thousand being armed with bow and arrow.

When he gives audience to his people, to listen to their complaints and set them to rights, he sits in a pavilion around which stand ten pages holding shields and gold-mounted swords; and on his right hand are the sons of the princes of the empire, splendidly clad and with gold plaited into their hair. The governor of the city is seated on the ground in front of the king, and all around him are his vizirs in the same position. The gate of the chamber is guarded by dogs of an excellent breed, who wear collars of gold and silver. The beginning of a royal audience is announced by the beating of a kind of drum which they call *deba*, made of a long piece of hollowed wood. The people gather when they hear this sound.

The King of Ghana exacts the right of one *dinar* of gold on each donkey-load of salt that enters his country. The best gold in the country comes from Ghiaru, a town situated in a country that is densely populated by Negroes and covered with villages. All pieces of gold found in the mines of the empire belong to the sovereign, although he lets the public have the gold dust that everybody knows about; without this precaution, gold would become so abundant as practically to lose its value.

*Al Bekri*

## 3 The Empire of Mali

The empire which Sundiata founded on his thirteenth-century conquests was to be much greater in extent than Ghana had been, and much wealthier. And while Ghana, in spite of the Almoravid conquest, was still mostly a heathen country, Mali was ruled by Moslems from the beginning. Many of its people became devout followers of the faith.

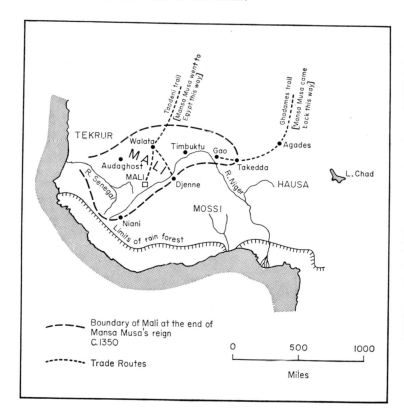

*The Empire of Mali*

Boundary of Mali at the end of Mansa Musa's reign C.1350

Trade Routes

0   500   1000

Miles

Origins

Little is known of Mali in the time before Sundiata. It began as a small Negro chiefdom on the Upper Niger to the south-west of Ghana. The chief's village was at Niani on the Sankara, a small tributary river. There was gold in the country. The long-established presence of Berber trading settlements perhaps explains why the people of Mali held to Islam after the Almoravid government was overthrown. It may also explain why the Sosso were jealous and afraid of the Mali kingdom of Kangaba.

## Sundiata

We have seen in the last chapter how Sundiata became the leader of this kingdom.

Sundiata is one of the great figures of history. Lame and sickly as a child, he had overcome his difficulties and had grown to manhood as a great warrior and hunter. So popular was he among the people, who knew that he was of royal descent, that he aroused the jealousy of the king. Fearing for his life, he went into exile, far away towards Timbuktu.

In 1240, however, oppressed by new threats from the Sosso, the king fled from Niani. Now the people called on Sundiata to come back and lead them.

As soon as he was back in Niani, Sundiata raised an army. Undeterred by grief at his mother's death on the eve of his departure, he marched north into the heart of Mandingo country. He was welcomed by the people as a liberator. Meeting Sumanguru and the Sosso on the decisive field of Krina, he won a complete victory. Sumanguru was taken captive, and died soon afterwards.

Before long, Kumbi was also taken, and Sundiata was proclaimed Emperor—no longer of Ghana, but of Mali. A new capital was made at Bamako, some way down the Niger from Niani, and Kumbi, already shattered by two conquests in ten years, fell into decay.

During the remaining fifteen years of his life, Sundiata's armies advanced the frontiers of his empire in every direction, especially down the Niger to the east, and down the Senegal to the west.

Sundiata died in 1255. He may have been shot by an arrow from an angry crowd, but others say he was accidentally drowned in the Sankara River.

## Islam in Mali

Though some of the people of Ghana had taken to Islam in Almoravid times, it was only now, under Sundiata and the other Moslem rulers who followed him, that the conversion became widespread.

The Mandingo and other Negro peoples of the Niger took to Islam with a fervour that amazed visitors from far afield. They were linked more and more closely with the rest of the Moslem world. There was the trade with the Berber states north of the desert. More directly, trade routes went to the eastern Sudan beyond the Shari. A few Moslems from Mali even used to make the pilgrimage to faraway Mecca. Indeed, Mali was no isolated state. One of the great empires of the whole world in its day, its people had a great sense of brotherhood with the rest of the Islamic world.

The most famous pilgrim from Mali to Mecca was the greatest of its rulers after Sundiata. This was Mansa Kankan Musa.

**Kankan Musa**

The ninth ruler of Mali after Sundiata, Musa was the great-grandson of the founder's sister. He ruled from 1307 to 1332. During his reign the frontiers of Mali were once again advanced, until the emperor's word was law as far as Cape Verde on the Atlantic coast. To the east, though resisted by the Mossi tribes of the Black Volta, Mali extended its power over the whole Niger bend, and even down the river beyond Gao.

When Kankan Musa made his pilgrimage to Mecca in 1324, he passed through Cairo. By this time, Cairo had grown to be more important than Baghdad, and was one of the great

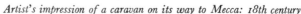

*Artist's impression of a caravan on its way to Mecca: 18th century*

*View of Cairo, showing the Citadel Mosque*

cities of the world. Even here, however, the size and the rich
finery of Musa's caravan made a powerful impression. The
people and rulers of Cairo marvelled at his retinue of sixty
thousand men, his eighty camels, each loaded with gold, and
the staves covered with beaten gold with which his five hundred
personal servants were equipped.

Musa's visit was talked about for years afterwards. It was the
first time that most people in Egypt realized that, beyond the
sunbaked and dusty plains of the central Sudan, there flowed
another great river, as great as the Nile; and that on its banks

there throve another kingdom rich in gold. What was more, marvel of marvels, its people were followers of the Prophet.

Because Cairo was a centre of Mediterranean trade, rumours of Mali reached Europe before long. The Empire of Mali is written on one of the earliest maps of Africa since Ptolemy, which was drawn by an Italian in 1375.

The pilgrimage to Mecca took three years. It is plain how well-governed Mali was, that its ruler could be away for so long. Meanwhile the armies of Mali continued their conquests. Musa returned to find that his general Sagama-Dir had captured Gao, the capital of the Songhai people, in 1325. Musa passed through Gao in triumph on his way home.

*A traveller's sketch of Timbuktu*

Impressed by what he had seen in Cairo and Mecca, Musa devoted the last years of his life to improving the cities of his country. The earliest flat-roofed brick-built houses were probably built in Timbuktu and Gao at this time, and new mosques were raised up. One, the Sankuru mosque at Timbuktu, was designed by Ishaq-es-Saheli, a Berber from southern Spain.

Originally a Tuareg settlement, Timbuktu had begun as a trading town. Situated at the northernmost point of the Niger bend, it has been called 'the port of the Sudan in the Sahara', where river canoe and desert camel meet. As formerly at Kumbi, gold from the south and salt from the north were exchanged in its markets. During the next century Timbuktu and another city called Djenne, farther up the Niger, became important centres of learning. We shall read of this in the next chapter, but their rise to greatness belongs to the days of the Empire of Mali.

Mansa Kankan Musa died in 1352. At the time of his death, Mali was at the height of its wealth and power. These rested on three things.

First of all, Mali controlled the richest gold deposits in West Africa. Now that the mines of Nubia, exploited for centuries by the Egyptians, were used up, the resources of the Niger-Senegal watershed were the richest of the known world. Gold from Mali found its way all over the Middle East and Europe. There the wars of the Cross had stimulated trade. The growth of towns in Europe during the Middle Ages was increasing the demand for gold.

Secondly, Mali now controlled the southern end of two of the great trans-Saharan camel trails, whereas Ghana had only controlled one. The first of these was the Taodeni trail, which went north through the western desert to Sijilmasa. On this route lay the rich salt mines of Taghaza oasis. There, salt was cut from the ground in blocks. It was even used to build houses. More or less independent, Taghaza was often in dispute between the Negro empires in the south and Morocco in the north. The real northern outpost of Mali was Walata. Here travellers coming south from Taghaza had to be met by guides before they were allowed to enter the town.

The other trail controlled by Mali at the southern end was the Ghadames trail from Tunis, through the Hoggar to Gao.

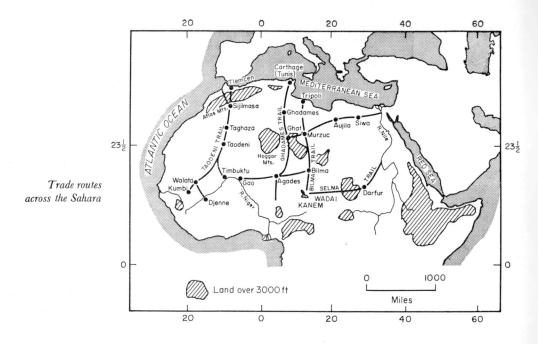

*Trade routes across the Sahara*

Lastly, the government of Mali was efficient and well-organized. Order and peace are essential if trade is to flourish. It is plain from Arab accounts that order and peace reigned in the Empire of Mali under Mansa Musa. The most important of these accounts was written by the great Arab geographer, Ibn Batuta.

**Ibn Batuta's account**

Ibn Batuta was a Moroccan Arab who travelled in many Moslem countries, writing about what he saw. He went to India and China as well as to Africa.

In 1352 he made a journey from Morocco to Mali, crossing the western Sahara from Sijilmasa to Walata. He spent three years in Mali, most of it in the capital, but he also visited Timbuktu and Gao.

Three things impressed Ibn Batuta. The first was the respect for law and order. The country was organized in provinces, each controlled by a governor or *Ferba*. Below him were *Mocrifs* who controlled towns and villages. Law was strictly enforced. 'The Negroes are of all peoples those who most abhor injustice,' wrote Ibn Batuta. Travellers could move about in safety. If one

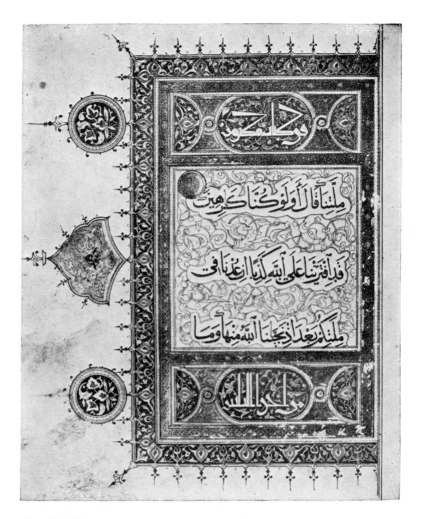

*A page of the Koran: Egyptian, 14th century*

should die, his goods were taken care of until someone came to claim them.

The second was the devoutness of the people, especially the wealthy and educated, in worshipping according to the faith of Islam. The mosques were full, and a worshipper who arrived late might not find a place. Clean white clothes were worn on Fridays, even by the poor. Children were made to learn the Koran by heart. There were, of course, many pagans in Mali, the Moslems being mostly in the big towns.

Lastly, Ibn Batuta noted the respect shown to the king or

*Mansa*, who was surrounded with great pomp. Audiences were held on a raised platform under a tree in the palace forecourt. The platform was carpeted with silk and covered with cushions. The king appeared, walking slowly, wearing a gold skull-cap and a red velvet tunic of cloth from Europe. In front came musicians with two-stringed guitars, and in the rear followed three hundred armed slaves. Drums, trumpets and bugles were sounded.

A subject who wished to see the king had to wear old clothes drawn up to the knees. He would approach, bowing low, and would knock the ground with his elbows. When spoken to by the king, he would throw dust over his back as a sign of submission.

Ibn Batuta saw how the Niger flowed eastwards, and wondered whether it later joined the Nile. When he returned home he drew a map showing the Empire of Mali; and after this, Mali appeared on European maps of the world until the sixteenth century.

## The decline of Mali

Although Ibn Batuta did not know it, Mali slowly began to decline in the years after his visit. No ruler as great as Musa succeeded to the throne. Soon there was a dispute between rival claimants, which led to civil war. A series of weak rulers followed. Gao claimed its independence. After 1400, Mali suffered increasingly from attacks by the Tuareg in the north, the Wolof in the west, and the Mossi in the south.

Finally the country was overthrown by the armies of Songhai in 1513. In the next chapter we shall read about the growth of this new and even greater empire.

# 4 Songhai

While first Ghana, and then Mali had been growing into strong states centred on the Upper Niger, another people had been building a new state along the Middle Niger.

These were the Negro people called the Songhai.

*The Empire of Songhai*

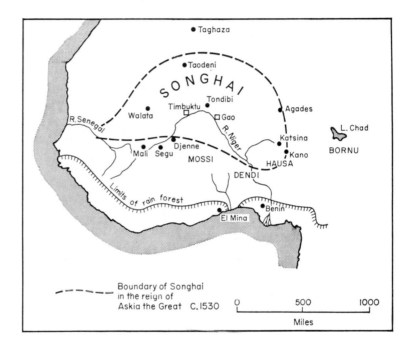

Boundary of Songhai in the reign of Askia the Great C.1530

0       500       1000
Miles

**How the Songhai kingdom began**

About the seventh century when, far up the Niger to the west, the kingdom of Ghana was growing strong under its first Berber kings, a Negro tribe called the Songhai moved from their homeland around the Bussa rapids, up to the Middle Niger.

From the rapids at Bussa in the east to Bamako in the west, the Niger flows through a thousand miles of dry, healthy country, without a single waterfall or rapid to break its even flow. It was to be the destiny of the Songhai to make this thousand miles their own.

The Songhai reached Gao about 650. There they found themselves at the southern end of the ancient cart trail through the Hoggar grasslands to Ghadames.

The Berbers of the Lemta tribe, who used this trail, fought the Songhai newcomers, and conquered them about 700. The Berber chief was called Za Aliamen. His descendants, called the Za kings, ruled the Songhai for over six hundred years. During this time, through intermarriage, they became partly Negro, and formed the Songhai into a strong nation.

In 1009, Za Kosoi became a Moslem, taught by Berber traders from the north. All the kings after him were Moslem, and the new religion slowly began to spread among the people.

**Mali conquers Songhai**

By this time Gao had become a large town, and its trade began to rival that of Timbuktu. At last, as we have seen, it was captured by Musa's army in 1325. The Za king was killed, and his two small sons were taken away as hostages.

For about fifty years, Gao and half the Songhai kingdom were ruled by the emperor of Mali. A palace and a fine new mosque were built in the town. But after Musa's death, the Songhai slowly stopped paying tribute to Mali. The two princes escaped from Timbuktu, and went back. The eldest started a new line of kings, giving up the old title of 'Za', and calling himself 'Sonni' instead.

Mali finally gave up Gao in 1435 because of Berber attacks. The Songhai managed to fight off the invaders, but the Berbers captured Timbuktu, and from this time Mali began to decline.

**Sonni Ali**

Mali's decline was Songhai's opportunity. The Negro peoples of the Niger did not like Berber rule. The rulers of Mali had not been able to keep the Berbers back, and now it was the turn of the Songhai.

In 1464 the governor of Timbuktu appealed to Gao for help in throwing off Berber rule. The king of Songhai at that time was Sonni Ali. When he reached Timbuktu he found that the Berbers had fled. The learned men of the schools and the university, however, made it clear that they feared the Songhai just as much, and did not want them in the city. This made Sonni Ali so angry that he destroyed many buildings, and hunted to death many of the citizens.

In fact Sonni Ali, though a great leader and fighter, was a hot-tempered and cruel man. Fortunately he had a wise general called Mohammed Ali Bekr, who knew how to wait until his master's temper had cooled before asking him a question.

Sonni Ali ruled from 1464 to 1492. After a siege of seven years, he also captured the other of Mali's university towns, Djenne. This time he treated the schoolmen more kindly. For a time, also, he held Walata in the desert. He even tried to build a canal from Lake Faquibine to Walata, but it was never finished. He fought long wars against the Mossi in the south and the Fulani in the north-east. When he died, the Songhai Empire was already stronger than Mali.

**Askia the Great**

Now Sonni Ali's great minister, Mohammed Ali Bekr, decided to make himself king. He fought and defeated Sonni Ali's sons, and rode back to Gao victorious. When told that Mohammed was now king, Sonni Ali's daughters in the palace cried out 'A si kyi a!'—'He isn't!' Mohammed heard of this and, laughing, declared that 'Askia' should be his title. So it was, and of the kings who followed him as well.

This man, even more than Mansa Musa of Mali, deserves the title of 'great'. Above all he was a great soldier. Attacking Mali in 1501, his armies conquered it after a long war, and extended the power of Songhai as far as the Atlantic coast where the Senegal and Gambia Rivers meet the sea. To the north he controlled for a time the salt mines of Taghaza, regarded for centuries by the Berbers as their own. To the east, he subdued the Hausa states around Katsina, and captured Kano (1513). He fought and conquered the Fulani and Tuareg of Aïr. A Negro colony at the Berber town of Agades survives to this day.

Besides this, however, Askia was a great administrator. He brought peace and good government to the whole of the western Sudan. The people of his cities had no fear of thieves; children could safely be sent to buy in the market; and travellers were safe on the road. Judges were honest and respected. Education was encouraged, and many books were bought and sold.

Lastly Askia, unlike Sonni Ali, was a strict Moslem. Wishing, perhaps, to do better than Musa a hundred and fifty years before, he made in 1495 a *hadj* or pilgrimage to Mecca. In his huge caravan were five hundred horsemen and a thousand foot soldiers, and his baggage train included three hundred thousand pieces of gold for expenses and gifts on the journey.

Askia Mohammed lived to be ninety-seven years old. He reigned for so long that his sons grew tired of waiting for their turn to rule. They rebelled against him in 1528, and Askia was exiled for three years. But the rebel princes could not govern well. Askia came back to Gao, and ruled until his death in 1538.

## The Moroccan wars

The kings after Askia Mohammed used the same title, but none was as capable. His sons quarrelled, until Askia Ishak I (1539–1549) restored order. With the death of Askia Daud in 1582, trouble broke out again.

Worst of all, war now began with Morocco across the desert. The Moroccans had long been waiting to seize the gold trade, and the quarrels in Songhai, together with a victory over their other enemies, the Portuguese, gave them their chance. In 1585 the great Shereef of Morocco, Muley Muhammed El Mansur, captured the salt mines of Taghaza. He then sent an army across the desert to attack Gao itself.

After the terrible desert journey of five months, only two thousand of the Moroccan army survived. None the less, in 1591 they defeated the Askia's army of twenty-eight thousand in the historic battle of Tondibi. Their victory was due to the use of firearms. It was the first time that gunpowder had been used in the Sudan. The fire-locks and muzzle-loading cannon, brought from Spain, were too much for the bows and arrows and spears of the Songhai.

*Tsetse-fly*

For twenty years the Shereef's army terrorized central Songhai. Gao was occupied, and Timbuktu was sacked, many of its books were destroyed and its educated men taken away to Marrakesh as slaves.

However, the war brought little profit to Morocco. The Moroccan army failed to reach the gold mines of Wangara and Asante. These lay in the forest belt, and in trying to find them, many soldiers died of malaria and dysentery, while their horses were killed by the tsetse-fly. It was difficult to send more soldiers across the desert.

In 1618 the Shereef of Morocco abandoned the Sudan.

## The end of the empires in the Sudan

The damage had been done; civilized government in Songhai had been destroyed. The Askias withdrew, with many of their own people of pure Songhai tribe, down the Niger to their own homeland in the Dendi region. The cities of Gao, Timbuktu and Djenne declined in importance.

The Moroccan soldiers stayed on the Niger and made

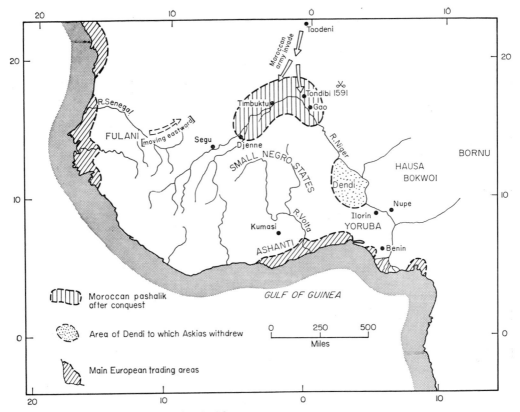

*West Africa in the 17th century after the Moroccan wars*

governments of their own, which lasted for one hundred and fifty years. But it was bad government: disorder and unhappiness returned to the country.

The battle of Tondibi therefore marked a turning point in the history of the Niger. The growth of civilization in the western Sudan was halted. Little progress was made in the next three hundred years. When the Scottish explorer Mungo Park journeyed down the Niger as far as Bussa in 1805, he found the country divided up into small states, often quarrelling with each other. The age of the great empires was over.

In the next two chapters we shall read of what had been happening in other parts of West Africa.

# West African Time Chart to 1600

| Date | Ghana | Mali | Songhai |
|------|-------|------|---------|
| **A.D.** | | | |
| 100 | Small Mandingo chiefdoms on Upper Niger and Senegal. | | |
| 200 | | | |
| 300 | | | |
| 400 | First Berber conquest. | Independent Mande tribes. | |
| 500 | | | |
| 600 | Second Berber conquest. | | Songhai Negroes move up Niger to Gao. |
| 700 | | | Berber conquest. Za kings begin. |
| 800 | Al Fazari calls Ghana 'land of gold' Revolution. Soninke kings begin. | Mali a small part of the Ghana kingdom. | |
| 900 | | | |
| 1000 | *Ghana kingdom at greatest extent.* Almoravid invasion. Ghana conquered 1069. | | Za kings converted to Islam. |
| 1100 | Islam in Ghana. Collapse of Almoravid rule. | | |
| 1200 | Sosso dominance under Sumanguru. End of Ghana. | Battle of Krina. Sundiata establishes Empire of Mali. | |
| 1300 | | Islam spreads along the Niger. | Gao conquered by Mali in 1325. |
| 1400 | | Musa's *hadj* to Mecca. Visit of Ibn Batuta (1352). *Greatest time of Mali's power and wealth.* | Songhai regains independence. |
| 1500 | | Songhai conquest. Collapse of Mali. | Sonni Ali creates Empire of Songhai. Askia conquers Mali. |
| 1600 | | | *Greatest extent of Songhai.* Moroccan wars. Collapse of Songhai. |

# 5 Kanem, Bornu and the Hausa states

In the last three chapters we have followed the rise and fall of three West African empires—Ghana, Mali and Songhai. These empires were centred on the Niger. Farther east meanwhile had grown the great kingdom of Bornu, which had grown out of the earlier state of Kanem. Bornu and Kanem were centred on Lake Chad.

Between Bornu and the Niger empires lay the Hausa states, which traded with these countries and also with North Africa, using the Ghadames trail.

We shall now see how Bornu and the Hausa states, which cover what is today Northern Nigeria, came into being.

**Kanem—an early kingdom of the Sudan**

From Chapter 8 in Book One you will remember how, during the last centuries B.C., Berber peoples from the north-east were moving west across the Tibesti Plateau towards Lake Chad. As the Sahara became dry, these Berbers sought for better grazing and water. They were pleased to find Lake Chad and the rivers flowing into it.

By A.D. 700 the Berbers, notably the Zaghawa, one of the strongest tribes, controlled the Sudan from Nubia in the east to Chad in the west. Around Lake Chad lived agricultural Negro people. The Berbers conquered them because, being nomads, they were better at fighting than the peaceful farmers.

Soon this huge, loose empire split up. About 800 one section, the Beni Sef, led by a chief called Dougou, founded the state of Kanem east of Lake Chad. Dougou's 'Sefawa' dynasty was to last a thousand years, so becoming one of the longest dynasties in the history of the world. The Beni Sef slowly intermarried with the Negro inhabitants, and Kanem became a Negro state. The title of the Kanem 'Sefawa' kings was *Mai*. Mai Selma (1193–1210) was the first Negro ruler of Kanem. He governed with a council of twelve, who were mostly members of the royal family.

Meanwhile, Islam was spreading through Egypt and North Africa. News of the new religion reached westward across the Sudan. In 1097 Mai Umme Jilmi became the first Moslem ruler of Kanem.

This was thirty years after the Almoravid conquest of

Ghana, far away to the west. The Niger states were converted to Islam from the north; the Chad states received it from the east.

## The growth of Bornu

Kanem was a large, unwieldy state. After 1200, when it reached its greatest extent under Mai Dunama Dibbalemi, there were quarrels and civil war. The people found it difficult to resist attacks by the Bulala, a Berber tribe of the central Sudan.

West of Lake Chad, however, was the country of Bornu. Bornu was friendly with the Hausa states; some historians even regard it as having been one of the Hausa states, about which we shall read below. To this country the Kanuri (people of Kanem) came in search of new lands. Already by 1200 the Mai sometimes used the title of 'King of Kanem and Master of Bornu'.

It took over a hundred years for the Sefawa kings to build their new state and establish peaceful government, but by the time of Mai Ali Gazi (1473 1501) it was done. Ali Gazi built a new capital at Ngazargamu, which you can see on the map.

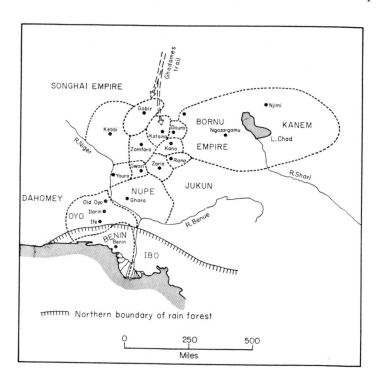

*Kanem, Bornu and the Hausa Bokwoi about 1550*

Thus by 1500 old Kanem east of Lake Chad no longer existed, and the strongest state in the Chad area was the Moslem kingdom of Bornu. Apart from Songhai, the last of the Niger empires, Bornu was the strongest kingdom in the whole of the western Sudan.

It was troubled, however, by the growing power of the Hausa states. We must now go back and see how these states had come into being.

**The Hausa states**

Some time around A.D. 800, which was the time when Ghana was beginning on the Upper Niger, and when Kanem was being formed under the Sefawa kings east of Chad, a group of towns grew up south of the desert between Lake Chad and the Niger bend.

This country was at the southern end of the Ghadames trail from Tunis. It was almost certainly for reasons of trade that these towns began. By 1200 there were seven of them, known as the Hausa Bokwoi. *Hausa* was the name of the language spoken by the people of these towns.

A legend says that Abuyazidu, a prince of Baghdad in far-off Persia (more probably he was the son of a Berber chieftain in eastern Bornu), quarrelled with his father and journeyed to western Bornu. At Daura he found that the people could not draw water because of a snake that lived in the well. Abuyazidu killed the snake. After that he married the Queen of Daura, and his six sons became the rulers of the other six Hausa towns. These were Kano and Katsina, trading communities; Zaria, a slave market; Rano, a craft centre; Gobir, a northern garrison against desert tribes; and Biram, between Kano and Lake Chad.

Although the story of the snake is a legend, these are the names of the original Hausa states. Probably the story represents an invasion of the Hausa country, led by a warrior called Abuyazidu, from ancient Bornu. Later new Hausa towns sprang up as trade increased. These were known as the Hausa Banza, and included Nupe, Yaura and even Ilorin, a Yoruba town south of the Niger.

**Kano**

The Hausa Bokwoi did not govern the people of the surrounding country. Each town had strong, high walls and mainly looked after its own defences and trade. Each was independent of the others, and there were sometimes wars between them.

*Scene at a gateway of the walled city of Kano, Nigeria*

The most important were Kano and Katsina, and by 1300 Kano was the strongest of all. Its king had a fine army, with mighty troops of horsemen.

This was the time when Mali was powerful on the Upper Niger. It was probably through the influence of Mali that some of the Hausa people were converted to Islam. We have read of Mansa Musa's pilgrimage to Mecca in 1325. He returned along the Ghadames trail. The Hausa were used to pilgrims. In fact Yaji, king of Kano in 1350, was a Moslem, although his successor was once more a pagan.

By 1400 Kano was a great city. Learned men from Mali went to stay there, and education spread among the wealthier people. Mosques were built. The law of the Koran was established, and the city was well governed.

Nevertheless, Islam was not so strongly established in the Hausa towns as it was in Mali and Songhai, or even in Bornu. From time to time the rulers were pagan, and many of the people were never Moslem. Pagan rites accompanied the enthronement of the Hausa kings. Indeed the Hausa, who occupy the north-west of modern Nigeria, were not properly converted to Islam until the Fulani *jihad* of the nineteenth century (see Chaper 15).

## Bornu and Songhai dominate Hausaland

By 1500, Songhai was a powerful empire on the Upper Niger. Bornu, as we have seen, was a great kingdom south-west of Lake Chad. Between them lay the rich Hausa towns. Clearly, both Bornu and Songhai would want to control the Hausa.

The Bornu attempt came first. Under Mai Idris (1507–29), Bornu conquered eastern Hausaland, and became its overlord. Each town had to pay taxes to the Mai every year.

Meanwhile Askia Mohammed of Songhai was advancing eastward from Gao. We have seen how in 1513 he subdued the western Hausa, and captured Katsina and Kano. The Hausa towns were left desolate by the invasion.

## The Hausa regain independence

Soon, however, the Hausa towns were able to throw off foreign domination. They succeeded for three reasons.

In the first place Askia the Great, blind at the end of his long reign, quarrelled with his sons. The governor of the Hausa town of Kebbi, who was called Kanta, took the opportunity to lead a Hausa revolt. Both the Songhai administrators and the Bornu tax-gatherers were driven out of Hausaland. Kanta, however, was killed fighting, and was unable to enjoy his triumph.

The second reason was the defeat of Songhai by the army of Morocco in 1591. We have read about the battle of Tondibi in the previous chapter. Songhai never recovered from this conquest, and the Hausa were thenceforth safe from attack in the west.

Thirdly, there took place the decline of Bornu. This did not happen at once. For a time Bornu recovered its power under Mai Idris Alooma. Greatest of the kings of Bornu, Idris Alooma had a fine army of noble cavalry. Both horses and men wore chain armour and brightly-coloured cloaks, and carried decorated shields and lances. Slaves and peasants, armed with spears and bows and arrows, came behind. With this well-trained force, Idris Alooma recovered power and reconquered Kano.

Forty years later, however, the kingdom of Bornu began to weaken under attacks of the Tuareg in the north and the Jukun in the south. The Jukun were a nomadic tribe who lived along the Upper Benue. Their raids troubled Bornu and Kanem until after 1700.

However, by the time that the rule of Bornu was thrown off by the Hausa, Kano was in decay after so many wars, and Katsina, now the strongest of the Hausa towns, controlled the Sahara trade.

Thus we see that the Hausa kept their independence in the end not so much through their own strength as because of the troubles and divisions of their enemies. They were good fighters, but they were never united enough to be a strong military power. They were still quarrelling among themselves when the force of the Fulani *jihad* (Chapter 15) broke upon them in 1804, and they were completely overrun.

*Hausa horsemen*

# 6 The forest kingdoms

South and west of the Lower Niger lies the country of the rain forest. This country was not reached by the power of Bornu to the north-east, or by that of the Hausa states to the north, or by that of Songhai to the north-west.

Thus the people who lived here were less influenced by Berber stock, and not at all by the Islamic religion. The kingdoms which developed around Ife, Oyo and Benin were Negro kingdoms. Even here, however, there were some contacts with foreign blood and culture.

*The forest kingdoms 1600–1800*

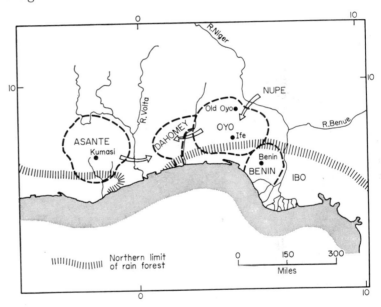

*The Yoruba*

Among the most numerous and important of the peoples living in the forest country by A.D. 1000 were the Yoruba.

We are not sure where the Yoruba came from. Like other peoples of the region, they have a tradition that they came from the east. They have some Hamitic blood, and it is likely that some of their ancestors were Berbers or Hamites from the Nile and perhaps, long before that, from Ethiopia and Arabia. These ancestors were, we believe, among those tribes which migrated west and south as the Sahara slowly dried up until, crossing the Shari River, they mixed with the Negro peoples of the western Sudan.

Some of these early Yoruba may have helped to form the Bantu-speaking peoples in their homeland in the Cameroons. They may be the ancestors of the Luba of the southern Congo.

The Yoruba of West Africa settled in the forest region of the Lower Niger about A.D. 1000. There, among the other Negro communities, whose language they now came to use, they founded the kingdom of Ile-Ife.

## Ile-Ife

*Brass head, probably representing an early Oni of Ife, and thought to date from the 13th or 14th century*

There are several legends of how this Yoruba state was founded. The most important tell of a founder chief called Oduduwa, who conquered the local inhabitants of Ile-Ife. His seven sons, says the legend, became the seven rulers of Yorubaland, who included the Alafin of Oyo and the Oba of Benin.

This is a story, but there is little doubt that the Yoruba at Ife did conquer the tribes round about, settle among them, and appoint new rulers. This happened during the three centuries from 1100 to 1400.

Ife, being the original town, was always looked upon by the Yoruba as their spiritual home. The Yoruba were gifted artists, and Ife became a centre for art and culture in this part of Africa. In recent years, several pieces of bronze sculpture and thousands of pieces of pottery have been unearthed near Ife. This craftwork was the result of two influences. First was the tradition of pottery manufacture among the local Negro peoples that had first flowered among the Nok community during the last centuries B.C. (see Chapter 9 of Book One). Second was the knowledge of brass-casting, developed on the Nile in the time of the Egyptian Empire. It may have been brought to West Africa by the ancestors of the Yoruba themselves.

The brass was cast by the 'lost-wax' method. Let us suppose that a head was to be made in brass. First, a model of the head was roughly prepared in clay. When this was dry, the head was covered by a coat of warm beeswax. The beeswax would of course cool and become hard. Then it was possible to scrape the details of the head on the surface of the wax. After that, the wax-covered model was again covered in clay, leaving a hole at the top and the bottom, and left to dry. Now the whole piece was baked hot. The wax ran out of the hole, leaving a space between the clay model and the clay covering. Into the hole at the top, molten brass was poured. When this had cooled hard, the outer layer of clay was broken away, leaving the brass model plain to see.

By 1300, brass-casting at Ife had reached a high standard, which was to some extent copied in other forest cities, notably Benin. When the Portuguese arrived two hundred years later, they were amazed at the quality of this craftsmanship. The bronzes of Ife are still among the finest pieces of sculpture in the world.

Oyo

Although Ife was the most cultured city in Yorubaland, Oyo was the most powerful.

Oyo was founded, says the legend, by Oranmiyan, a prince of Ife. The Edo people of Benin to the south-east were in trouble. They asked the Oni of Ife, whom they respected, to send a member of the Ife royal family to be their ruler. Oranmiyan was sent, but he did not like living among the Edo of Benin. After a short time he left and founded his own town at Oyo, about fifty miles north of Ife. This happened in about 1250.

Oyo was situated in the northern fringe of the forest, with more open grassland suitable for horses. In subsequent years the Alafin (ruler) of Oyo was able to develop a strong army, and by using cavalry—armed horsemen—he succeeded in repelling enemies such as the Nupe north of the Niger. He made his capital the centre for the trade that came southward to the forest belt from Hausaland in the north.

As a result, the Alafin of Oyo became the strongest ruler in Yorubaland. His power extended from the Niger in the north-east to Togoland in the west. To the south it was bounded by the region of the mangrove forest. Even Ife submitted to the rule of Oyo, although the people of Oyo still looked on the Oni of Ife as their spiritual leader.

The system of government in Oyo was remarkable. The Alafin was not all-powerful, and he had to show responsibility towards his people. He was chosen from among members of the royal family by a council of seven notables called the Oyo Mesi. If he used his power wrongly, he could be presented by the Basorun, leader of the Oyo Mesi, with an empty calabash which was a sign that he had to kill himself. 'The gods reject

47

*Ivory pendant, probably representing an Oba of Benin*

you, the people reject you, the earth rejects you,' he would be told.

Below the royal family, the palace officials and the Oyo Mesi were the army leaders. These were not hereditary, but were appointed by the Alafin. The Kakanfo, or army commander, was not allowed to lose a battle. If defeated, he had to take his own life. For this reason Oyo generals were usually successful. Some who suffered defeat went away to form new Yoruba communities elsewhere rather than return home.

The Alafin who began the expansion of the Oyo Empire, a successor of Oranmiyan, was a famous ruler named Shango. There is a story about him that he liked to use magic. One day, to show his power, he used it to call down lightning. The lightning struck his house and killed his wives and children. Stricken with grief, the king took his own life.

Though Oyo was not as large an empire as Mali and Songhai to the north, it grew to be a powerful state. Wars were fought against the Hausa Banza of Nupe across the river, and once the Yoruba were severely defeated. They were saved, however, by the leadership of a brilliant general, Ofonran, and the armies of Nupe were driven out. By 1600 the power of Oyo was at its greatest extent. Later, in the eighteenth century, even Dahomey was conquered and ruled for a short time.

## The end of the Yoruba Empire

However, this large area, much of it in the rain forest with poor communications, was too large for the rulers of Oyo to govern properly. After about 1750, the empire began to break up. There were three reasons.

First, the more distant parts began to demand independence. In 1789 the King of Dahomey refused to pay tribute any more.

The second reason was the slave trade with the Europeans on the coast. This was increasing in the eighteenth century, and for this and other reasons the old trade with the north was declining. However, Oyo was too far north to gain much from the slave trade, and so became poorer and less important than other centres nearer the coast.

Thirdly, some of the leading subjects of the Alafin began to rebel against him. In a civil war which began in 1820, the Kakanfo Afonju, in particular, used the help of the Fulani, recent conquerors of the Hausa, to overthrow the Alafin Aole.

The Fulani then turned on Afonju, who was killed in battle,

and occupied Ilorin, a northern outpost of Oyo, and prevented the Yoruba from taking slaves from north of the Niger. The Yoruba had to have slaves to sell to the European traders, so they began to fight among themselves. Even Ife, the original home of the Yoruba, was now destroyed. In 1837 Oyo was moved south to a new site nearer the coast. Ibadan, however, between Oyo and Lagos, became the most important town.

Although the Yoruba, from their new centre in the forest, managed to keep the Fulani at bay, they were thus in a weak and divided condition when European traders and missionaries came inland in the late nineteenth century.

## Benin

Meanwhile, to the south-east between the coast and the lower Niger, another kingdom had been flourishing, whose centre was the city of Benin.

The traditions of the Bini—that is, the Edo people of Benin—say that, like the Yoruba of Ife, their ancestors came long ago from the far-off Nile. The first dynasty at Benin, supposed to have been descended from the gods, was founded about A.D. 900. At this time the kings were called *Ogieso*, which means 'ruler of the sky'.

About 1160 the king, Osogau, was banished for misgovernment. For some years Benin was a republic. Eventually it was decided to return to monarchy, and Oduduwa, the Oni of Ife, was invited to send one of his sons to be ruler of Benin. Oranmiyan was sent.

Oranmiyan, as we have seen, did not want to continue living at Benin. Before he left, however, he married a princess of Benin, and their son now became the new Oba, with the title of Eweka I. This dynasty has continued to the present day.

The rulers of Benin, therefore, were now related to the rulers of Ife. For a long time they recognized this link. When the Oba of Benin died, the Oni of Ife would send his successor a sculptured brass head. However, another account says that he used to send a staff and a brass helmet. This was a sign that Benin was dependent on Ife, but by 1500 it had shaken off this dependence.

## Brass-casting at Benin

About 1300 the wise Oba Oguola greatly admired the brass ornaments that were sent to him from Ife. Wanting to introduce the art to his own country, he asked for a craftsman to be

(left)
*Bronze plaque from Benin,
probably depicting
a Portuguese soldier*

(right)
*Bronze figure of a hunter
carrying an antelope*

sent. The man who came was Iguegha, a fine brass-smith who taught the people of Benin to cast brass by the lost-wax method.

The brass-smiths were strictly controlled by the Oba. The technique was kept secret. The craftsmen lived in a special street in the city called Igueroyo, after the name of the smith sent from Ife.

Before long the brasswork of Benin was as fine as that of Ife. It was greatly admired by the Portuguese when they visited the city after 1472.

**Benin grows powerful through trade**

When the Portuguese and other Europeans came to the coast after 1472, Benin began to grow wealthy. Lying midway between the Niger and Lagos—a coast town which the Edo of Benin claim to have founded—they were in a good position for trade. They bought European goods for themselves, and also for sale to the Yoruba inland. At this time guns and powder, and also fruits like pawpaws and coconuts, first entered the country. To the European traders the Edo exported pepper, ivory, palm-oil, cotton and—increasingly—slaves.

Being fairly near to the sea, Benin was visited by Portuguese, Dutch and English traders. From the accounts of these men we know something of what Benin was like.

It was a large city surrounded by fortifications which extended for 28 miles. By the sixteenth century it had a population of several thousand. A high wall and a deep ditch surrounded the city, the entrances to which were guarded by strong wooden gates. A Dutch visitor in 1602 described thirty main streets, each a hundred and thirty feet wide. Houses were well-built with spacious verandas. Cooking was done inside the house, a hole in the roof permitting the smoke to escape. The Oba lived in a fine palace or *eguae* built between the two west walls of the city.

The city was kept clean, and well-established laws were enforced by the Oba's police. Life was not always easy or pleasant, however. Many slaves were kept, who were killed when their master died. Human sacrifices were carried out according to the rites of the pagan religion.

By 1650, Benin was at the height of its prosperity and power. A century later, however, its power and influence were gone.

The main reason for this decline was the slave trade (see Chapter 8). The Obas grew rich on this trade, and government went from bad to worse as they grew more corrupt. Wars— sometimes civil wars—were fought to gather slaves for sale.

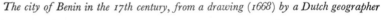

*The city of Benin in the 17th century, from a drawing (1668) by a Dutch geographer*

The country round Benin became empty of people. Life became insecure, farming was ruined, and interest in art declined.

Meanwhile other states were having more success, and taking the trade from Benin. To the west, as we have seen, were the Yoruba. To the east, across the Niger, other tribes, notably the Ibo, were becoming powerful.

## East of the Niger

While the Yoruba and Edo peoples, about whom we have been reading, had been settling west of the Niger, other Negro communities had crossed the Benue and settled east of the river, between the Benue, the Niger and the Cameroon Highlands.

The earliest of these settlers are believed to have been the Ijaw, who today live in and around the delta. They have a very old language. Probably they arrived about A.D. 1000 and became a river people, skilled at fishing and building canoes. Later they traded across the Niger with the city of Benin.

Another early group of settlers were the Ibibio. They lived farther east, between the Cross River and the Cameroons Mountain in the country known as Calabar. Later they traded with the Portuguese, who found the Cross River a useful inland waterway for their ships.

The Ijaw and the Ibibio had been pushed south by a strong tribe to the north of them—the Ibo. The Ibo were the most numerous of the people east of the Niger. Energetic and independent-minded, they did not like to have a strong chief or 'divine king' such as ruled in Oyo and Benin. Therefore they had no big capital city, but lived in small towns and villages all over Iboland. However, they believed in a supreme god, to whom they spoke through an oracle, 'Chukwu', who belonged to the Aro clan and became very important and wealthy, by selling advice about matters such as trade and war.

The Ibo, indeed, became great traders. They traded both with Benin across the Niger and, through the delta peoples, with the Europeans on the coast. Their main export was slaves. By 1600 they were growing fruits such as pineapple and pawpaw which had been brought to Africa by the Portuguese. By 1700 they were buying gunpowder, iron bars and cloth from African traders who came up from the coast. In exchange they sold slaves and rare woods. In the end they became the most numerous and powerful people in what was to become the eastern region of Nigeria.

# 7 Kingdoms of the Congo

To the east of the rain forests of the Niger delta stand the mountains and hills of the Cameroon Highlands. In this grassy hill country the Negroes of the west and the Hamites of the east had met and mingled in the centuries of Meroe and its decline. During the five centuries before and after the beginning of our era, the Bantu-speaking peoples had been formed.

Some of these energetic, iron-working people had, as we have seen, moved eastward to the Congo Highlands and the lake region of East Africa. Others moved south into the hills of Gabon between the Congo basin and the sea. A few moved into the forests of the Congo basin itself. There they found it easy, with their iron weapons, to drive out the Pygmies they found living there. Not many did this, however; it was difficult to grow food in the thick Congo forest.

In this chapter we shall follow the story of three African kingdoms that were formed in the more open country to the south of the Lower Congo—those of the Kongo, the Kuba and the Luba peoples. Here the forest opens out into grassland and plateau. From this plateau the southern tributaries of the Congo River come.

## The kingdom of Kongo

Little is known of the early history of the Kongo before the Portuguese came. Arriving from the north, where they had made their way through the rain forest, by 1300 the Kongo were the strongest tribe between the Kwango River and the sea. Their capital was at Mbanza. This was about a hundred miles south of where Kinshasa is today.

Most tribes in the region were early Bantu settlers who were without chiefs. The Kongo, however, had a system of rule by chiefs. At first the ruler was not very powerful. A new chief was not always the eldest son, and he often had to fight for his rights against rival members of the royal family. However, by 1400 the power of the king was increasing; so too was the size of the kingdom. It extended to the Kwango River in the east and to the Bengo River, which flows into the Atlantic near Luanda, in the south. There were six provinces. Each was controlled by a strong governor, or sub-chief. Each governor sent a tribute of raffia and cowrie shells to the king every year.

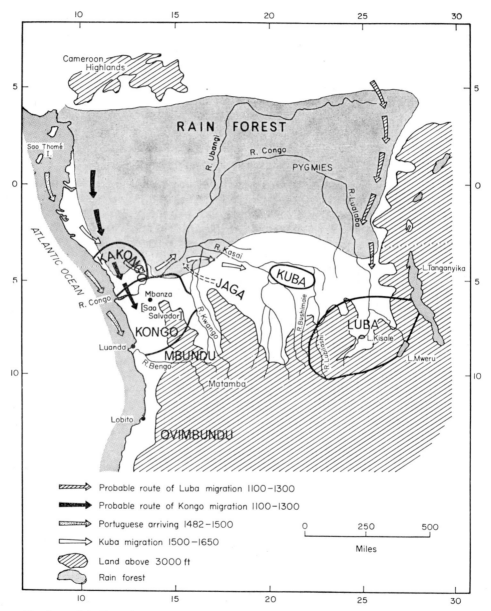

Map labels:

Cameroon Highlands

Sao Thomé I.

RAIN FOREST

R. Ubangi
R. Congo
PYGMIES
R. Lualaba

ATLANTIC OCEAN

R. Congo

R. Kasai

KAKONGO

JAGA

KUBA

L. Tanganyika

Mbanza [Sao Salvador]

KONGO

R. Kwango

R. Bushimaie

LUBA
L. Kisale

R. Lubilashi

L. Mweru

Luanda

MBUNDU

R. Bengo

Matamba

Lobito

OVIMBUNDU

Legend:

▨▶ Probable route of Luba migration 1100–1300

◼▶ Probable route of Kongo migration 1100–1300

▨▶ Portuguese arriving 1482–1500

▷ Kuba migration 1500–1650

▨ Land above 3000 ft

⬡ Rain forest

Scale: 0    250    500 Miles

*Kingdoms of the Congo basin 1300–1600*

The king, or Mani-Kongo, also received tribute from some of the tribes to the north of the river.

Raffia is a fibre made from palm leaves. The Kongo were skilful at weaving it into cloth and mats with ornate patterns. This weaving was greatly admired by the Portuguese when they first came to the country. Cowrie shells were obtained from the sea, especially from near Luanda. They were used as money in this part of Africa, as also, in Book One, we found them being used by the Arabs on the east coast. The Kongo did not know about gold, and when the Portuguese came and offered gold presents, the Africans refused them, demanding cowrie shells instead.

Although the Kongo had no knowledge of gold, they knew how to make copper and, of course, iron. There was iron in the hill country around Mbanza, and this was what made the Kongo into a more powerful tribe than their neighbours. With iron hoes they cultivated millet and sorghum. Fruits grew abundantly in the forest. There were no cattle here, but meat was obtained by hunting.

*The ruins of Sao Salvador*

*Congo forest*

**Portuguese influence**

It was at this time, when the Kongo kingdom was becoming an organized state, that Portuguese sailors in 1482 reached the mouth of the Congo River. Diego Cao, the Portuguese captain, was impressed with the size and power of the Kongo state. He persuaded the King of Portugal to make an alliance with the Mani-Congo Nzinga Nkuwu, who accepted missionaries and teachers. Nzinga's son was baptized and later became King

Afonso I. A church was built at Mbanza, which was renamed Sao Salvador.

All this, however, did the Kongo more harm than good. Kongo chiefs became jealous of Portuguese influence and rebelled against the king. In 1526 Afonso appealed to Portugal for help, but none came, because Portugal now had many other trading posts to think about, especially in India and the Far East. The Portuguese planters on Sao Thomé Island began to buy slaves in Kongo country for work on their plantations. The Kongo government tried to stop this but were unable to do so, because the chiefs wanted Portuguese cloth and guns so badly that they were prepared to capture people and sell them as slaves in order to obtain these articles.

By 1600 the Kongo state had split up into parts which were frequently at war with one another.

**Angola**

The story was much the same in the highlands of Angola, farther south. There the strongest tribe was the Mbundu, who had arrived from the west and made themselves powerful over earlier Bantu settlers, just as the Kongo had done to the north of them.

The ruler of the Mbundu had the title of Ngola, which is why the Portuguese gave this name to the country. The Portuguese were sure there were silver mines in Mbundu country. There were even stories that silver grew on the trees. Finding none, the Portuguese took slaves instead. The Mbundu therefore retreated inland to Matamba. They fought repeatedly against the invaders under leaders of whom the heroic Queen Nzinga (c. 1580–1663) is the best known.

The Portuguese kept control of the Angola coast and of their trading posts like Luanda and Lobito. The Mbundu and other tribes kept their independence till the nineteenth century. But wars and slave trading had once again weakened the authority of rulers, and stopped the growth of an organized African state.

**The Kuba**

Foreign influence could not, however, damage the growth of two important kingdoms far inland. The first of these belonged to the Kuba tribe in the southern Congo, who built a powerful state east of the Kwango River, among the tributaries of the Kasai.

At first the Kuba had lived in Gabon, north of the Congo

*The 17th century church of Nazare in Luanda, Angola*

River. When the Portuguese arrived and began to trade for slaves after 1500, the Kuba left their villages and travelled inland. They crossed the great river in canoes and settled on its south bank, living by fishing and hunting.

One hundred years later a wandering tribe of brigands, the Jaga, came marauding from the south-east, and drove out the Kuba. The Kuba took to their canoes, and escaped up the Kasai River. Finally they settled in more open country between the Kasai and Sankuru Rivers.

When they arrived there, the Kuba were still a small tribe of hunters and fishermen. From the Gabon they brought the knowledge of copper and iron working. Among the people of their new country they now learnt to cultivate millet. They did not weave raffia as the Kongo did, but made their clothes from bark cloth.

**The Bushongo lead the Kuba**

A leading Kuba tribe was the Bushongo clan. During their migration up the Kasai, they had appointed a 'captain of canoes'. Upon arrival in the new country, this man continued to act as chief of the clan. He must have been a capable leader, for when he died the Bushongo headmen elected one of his sons to succeed him. At first the system of election was customary, and an unpopular chief could be deposed. Before long, however, the position of chief became hereditary.

Now the Bushongo invented new ceremonial, and treated their kings with growing respect. Each local chief had to take an oath of allegiance at the beginning of a reign, and was obliged to present the new king with a wife as a token of his loyalty. Councils of elders were appointed among the subject tribes, and ministers controlled different departments of government. Tribute was paid annually. In fact, a powerful new state was growing along the Upper Kasai.

**Shyama Ngoongo**

Other Kuba tribes, however, were jealous of the power wielded by the Bushongo. Some time about 1750, a revolution occurred. The Bushongo king was killed, and his place was taken by a Kuba adventurer from the west named Shyama Ngoongo.

Shyama had lived on the Kwango River, and knew the customs of the Bakongo and other tribes in the west. Despite his adventurous career, he now proved himself one of the steadiest and wisest of African kings. To the Kuba he brought craftsmen who taught them how to weave raffia, and also the art of woodcarving. This art became highly developed, so that Kuba woodcarving is among the finest in Africa. Shyama also taught his people how to grow maize, groundnuts and tomatoes, crops which the Portuguese had brought to Africa from Brazil. Trade increased. The Kuba traded with the Portuguese on the west coast, and with the Bantu of the Congo Highlands in the east. They were becoming peaceful, wealthy and powerful.

Kuba power was exercised wisely. Subject tribes were allowed to govern themselves, provided they paid the annual tribute taxes. Shyama, however, made sure of his strength by making his capital into a large town. There the young men were trained to serve in a standing army.

Shyama, the wise king, was regarded with great reverence by the Kuba people. Legends grew up that his ancestors were descended from the gods. Other African tribes of the southern Congo, such as the Luyi and the Bemba, have legends like this. They were in fact inventing a kind of 'divine kingship'. It is interesting that this happened because these Bantu states were a long way from the Sudanic kingdoms in the north.

Meanwhile a third great Congo kingdom had been growing up still farther east, on the northern part of the plateau which today we call Katanga. This was the Luba Empire.

We are not sure where the Luba came from. Because of the name (Luba=Ruba), some people have thought they were connected with the early Yoruba long ago. Certainly we know that they came from the north, perhaps moving up the valley of the Upper Congo River, or possibly along tributaries of the Kasai.

By 1300 there was a Luba kingdom on the Upper Lualaba River. A burial ground of that date has been found along some miles of river bank on the Upper Lualaba near Lake Kisale. In the graves have been found copper goods, and among them some H-shaped copper bars such as the Luba are known to have made.

Luba traditions say that this early kingdom was ruled by chiefs of the Songye clan, a strong tribe to the north. In about 1500, however, there was a revolt. The Luba drove out their Songye rulers and set up a new Luba Empire. It extended from Lake Tanganyika to the Upper Kasai.

To the south of this Luba Empire lay the region of present-day Katanga. Here lived the Lunda tribe. In about 1600 a Luba prince called Ilunga made a marriage alliance with the Lunda Queen, Lueji. Their descendants, the Lunda emperors, were independent of the Luba. They were known by the title of *Mwata Yamvo*, which means 'Lord of Wealth'. This wealth lay in ivory and copper which were both in abundant supply, and which the Mwata Yamvos traded to the Portuguese in the west and later to the Arabs in the east. They also traded, as we have seen (see Chapter 12, Book One), with Monomotapa's kingdom south of the Zambezi.

We shall read more about this Lunda Empire in Chapter 11.

# 8 New trade comes to West Africa

In the last two chapters, mention has several times been made of the Portuguese. This is natural, because after 1480 the Portuguese had a considerable effect on the inhabitants of the West African coast, and of the Congo basin and Angola. In the next two chapters we turn to look more closely at the arrival of the Portuguese and of other European traders.

We shall begin by taking a look at the inhabitants of the west coast at that time. The Empires of Mali and Songhai, described in previous chapters, had flourished along the Niger River. The kingdoms of the Asante and of Dahomey and Oyo had been centred on the northern fringe of the rain forest. Of the largest West African states, only Benin had extended its power as far as the sea.

*Map to illustrate the early European trade on the West African coast 1500–1800*

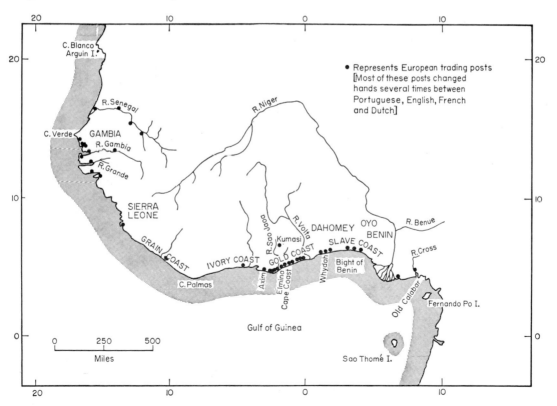

In the coastal forest belt between Cape Verde and the Niger delta lived Negro peoples. These Negroes, as we saw in Chapter 8, Book One, had slowly been driven south and west by stronger tribes from the north ever since 5000 B.C. Most of them occupied their present homes long before the beginning of our era.

By A.D. 1400 most of these west coast African tribes knew how to smelt iron. Several had discovered the value of ivory and of gold which they exported to the empires of the Niger. Some of this gold, as we have seen, found its way across the Sahara to the Berbers in the north, and to Europe.

## The west coast

Let us look more closely at the west coast as far as the Bight of Benin. It can be divided into four parts. First is the stretch around Cape Verde, including the Senegal and Gambia Rivers. We call this region Senegambia. Inland were the peoples of Tekrur, whom we have already met. The strongest coast tribes were the Jalofo and the Kantora.

South of Senegambia is the coast between the mountains of Sierra Leone and Cape Palmas. Inland here lived the Sosso, who had taken refuge in the hills after Sundiata of Mali had driven them away from the Upper Niger in 1240. Along the coast lived the Bullom and the Temne peoples, who had arrived there long before.

East of Cape Palmas lies the third stretch of coast, centred on the Volta River. Because of the rich gold trade which developed here later, this came to be known to Europeans as the Gold Coast. Inland, in the hill country to the west of the Volta, lived the Asante tribe. These were members of the Akan group of peoples who, as we have seen, came down from the north about 1100. Along the coast lived a number of tribes, of whom the strongest were the Nzima and the Fante (both related to the Akan group), the Ga and the Ewe. Many of these coast people were keen fishermen. They also traded sometimes with the Asante and tribes inland.

Farther east still is the fourth part of the coast, from the Bight of Benin to the Niger delta. From here the European traders obtained the biggest supply of slaves, so that it came to be known as the Slave Coast. Inland were the strong states of Togo, Dahomey, Oyo and Benin. Yoruba and Edo peoples also dominated the sea coast.

## The coast peoples

The tribes along the coast were many. We have only given the names of a few. They had different ways of life. Some, like the Asante and the Ga, had strong chiefs. Others had no proper chiefs at all, and just lived in groups of huts under headmen.

There was no unity among these tribes, and they spoke different languages. They continued to respect the forest gods because the Moslem missionaries seldom tried to settle in the unhealthy forest belt. Some Moslems were working along the Gambia River by 1400, but that was all. Thus there was no learning along the coast. Except for a small amount of trade inland, the coast peoples were isolated.

Then, in the fifteenth century, a change came from an unexpected direction—the sea.

## The Portuguese

*Prince Henry the Navigator*

One morning in 1445 the people of Cape Verde were astounded to see a strange ship, a caravel, with two masts and triangular sails, lying off the shore. From it came a small boat, rowed by men with long dark hair and light skins. Stepping ashore, the leader persuaded the watching Africans to take him to the local chief's village.

There the stranger introduced himself as Nuna Tristao. He came from Portugal, and had been sent by Prince Henry, a son of the king.

Henry the Navigator, as the prince was called, had heard of West African gold from the Berbers of the Mahgrib. He thought it might be possible to trade with West Africa by sea, instead of by crossing the desert as the Berbers had always done. After founding a sailing school at Sagres in Portugal in 1419, Prince Henry had sent ship after ship to try and find the way round the Guinea coast—*Guinea* was the Portuguese word for 'land of the black people'. Nuna Tristao was one of the prince's captains.

After Nuna had explained all this to the people of Cape Verde, he made a treaty of friendship with them and sailed home. Three years later he returned and sailed as far as the Rio Grande, fifty miles south of the Gambia, but there the people were not so friendly, and he was killed as he came ashore.

## Diego Gomes

Meanwhile Prince Henry was sending out more caravels. In 1458 Diego Gomes sailed along the Gambia River as far as

*A Portuguese caravel,*
*from a 16th century drawing*

Kantora. The people there told Diego of rich gold-mines farther up-river, but he decided it was safer to return. His voyage was not wasted, for he obtained 180 lb of gold from an African chief on the north bank, and a gift of ivory and slaves from the Jalofo. Another chief, Numimansa, asked for a Christian missionary to be sent, and next year Prince Henry sent an abbot, who built a little church at Juffure. This was the first Christian church in tropical Africa.

Prince Henry died in 1460. His life's work had seen the beginning of European activity in West Africa, including trade in gold and ivory, missionary work and slave trading.

**Further voyages**

The Portuguese, encouraged by their king, continued to explore the west coast. In 1462 Pedro da Sintra made a map of the coast of Sierra Leone. Nine years later, two captains sent by Fernao Gomes discovered the mouth of the Sao Jaoa River (or Pra River). Fernao Gomes had been given the monopoly of the Gold Coast trade for five years, but after that the Portuguese government took direct control. In 1481, resolving to profit from the rich gold in the area, the Portuguese built Elmina Castle twenty miles farther east of the river mouth.

The following year, in 1482, Diego Cao sailed right along the coast, and south as far as the mouth of the Congo River. By this time the Portuguese were hoping to find a sea route round Africa to India. Stories that this would be possible had

*Sierra Leone coastline today*

come to them from Pedro Covilhao, a traveller in Ethiopia. In the next chapter we shall read how they succeeded in doing this.

Meanwhile Portuguese caravels were coming, sometimes singly, sometimes two or three at a time, to the Guinea Coast every year. Many trading posts were set up, and plantations were also begun on the islands of Sao Thomé and Fernando Po.

**Other countries send ships**

Other European countries soon heard of the Portuguese success. At first, Spanish ships started to come for slaves; but in 1480, by the Treaty of Tordesillas, the King of Spain recognized the Portuguese monopoly in West Africa.

Instead, the Portuguese soon had to face competition from the French and the English. In 1492 a French ship captured a Portuguese vessel laden with gold bound from Elmina to Lisbon. Such fights were frequent. Forts like Elmina, in fact, were built less for protection against Africans than for defence against foreign ships. Between 1500 and 1600, French and English 'sea-dogs' captured many Portuguese ships and took their gold.

*The fortress of Elmina as seen from the lagoon*

By this time the Portuguese were also busy in Brazil, and in Mozambique, about which we shall read in the next chapter, and in India. They began to lose their hold on the Guinea Coast of Africa. By 1600 the French had their own trading stations north of the Gambia. The English had stations on the river itself, and two English trading companies sent ships regularly to the west coast. After 1600, Dutch sailors also joined in. The Dutch captured Elmina Castle from the Portuguese in 1637.

**Trading companies**

After the Portuguese, the Europeans who set up forts and trading posts were not sent by their governments, but by trading companies. These companies were of course encouraged by their governments, who took part of the profit. In 1561, for

*Christiansborg Castle under the British flag*

example, the 'Company of Merchant Adventurers for Guinea' was formed in London. Other companies followed. The most famous of all was the 'Royal Adventurers of England Trading into Africa', formed in 1660. In the same way the French, the Dutch, the Danes and the Swedes all had trading companies.

All these companies built forts, which were abandoned, sold, attacked, captured or exchanged from time to time. Some were strong castles like Elmina, Cape Coast and Christiansborg in present-day Ghana. Others were quite small and had only one or two Europeans to defend them.

A company which built a trading post or a fort paid rent for it to the local African chief. The rent for Elmina Castle was two ounces of gold a month. Cape Coast paid four ounces a month. The Europeans did not claim land or try to rule the Africans until after 1880.

The Europeans did not often travel inland; instead the Africans came to the coast to trade with them. The chief reason for this was malaria, a disease the Europeans did not understand, but which killed many. They did, however, sail up the Senegal and Gambia Rivers, which were deep enough for their ships.

## The slave trade

Quite soon after they began coming to West Africa the European traders found that gold and ivory and other African goods did not by themselves make enough profit. Therefore they began to take slaves as well. The Portuguese, as we have seen, took slaves from the Jalofo of Gambia as early as 1458, though this was a gift. Soon more were being taken in exchange for money or goods.

In the next century, plantations and mines were started in the West Indies, Brazil and Central America. Because the climate in those places was too hot and humid for Europeans to work in, many more slaves were now needed.

John Hawkins, an Englishman, was one of the first big slave traders. In 1562 he made his first slave trading voyage. He took Africans to the West Indies and Spanish America, where he sold them for hides, sugar and silver. These he took and sold in England. He became a rich man.

The Portuguese, however, were the main slave traders in the sixteenth century. Between 1530 and 1560 they carried 900,000 slaves across the Atlantic. But the other trading companies joined in. Altogether between 1500 and 1864 about twenty million Africans were taken from West Africa to the New World. That is why there are so many people of African descent in South America, the West Indies and the United States of America today.

It is true that the Africans had slaves in their own communities, but they were usually well treated as members of the family. Sometimes they were sold to the Berber traders across the Sahara. Even this was different from being captured, sold, taken on a terrible sea voyage, and often harshly treated in a strange land from which there was no return.

African chiefs took a leading part in the trade. The King of Dahomey was one of the greatest slave traders, and Europeans used to come to his town to do business with him. Farther west, on the other hand, along the Gold Coast, African traders acting as middlemen obtained slaves inland and brought them down to the coast for the European traders to buy.

**Effects of this early foreign trade**

Trade is usually good for mankind: it makes possible the exchange of ideas as well as of goods, so it causes civilization to spread. Wealth is increased, and with it opportunities for leisure and education.

Early European trade in West Africa did not have this effect. West Coast peoples had always been poor, and had sometimes fought one another for land or food. Wars now became more frequent, but wealth did not increase. Europeans used the help of African chiefs in fighting other Africans or against other companies. Guns came to be commonly used.

It was worse in the interior. Strong tribes like the Asante became stronger and raided other tribes for slaves. Formerly the chief had been the voice and servant of the people. Now chiefs became powerful despots like the King of Dahomey. European goods did little to improve African life. On the other hand the loss of young men and women ruined the villages.

Few missionaries came to teach the people. The Portuguese, it is true, sent missionaries in the sixteenth century to the Kongo, and also to Monomotapa in Mashonaland. In each of these states there were some Christian rulers for a time. However, the mission work was spoilt by the ambition of traders and not supported enough from Europe. Portugal became too interested in her colonies in the Far East and gave up many of her African trading posts. On the West African coast, except for the Gambia and Senegal settlements, there was no missionary work at all.

Not until the slave trade ended in the nineteenth century did West Africa begin to benefit from European trade. This was to begin in the oil palm region of the Niger delta.

## The West Coast slave trade

*An African protest*

Moreover, Sir, in our kingdoms there is another great inconvenience which is of little service to God, and this is that many of our people, keenly desirous as they are of the wares and things of your kingdoms, which are brought here by your people, and in order to satisfy their voracious appetite, seize many of our people, freed and exempt men; and very often it happens that they kidnap even noblemen and the sons of noblemen, and take them to be sold to the white men who are in our kingdom. And as soon as they are taken by the white men they are immediately ironed and branded with fire.

That is why we beg of Your Highness to help and assist us in this matter, commanding your traders that they should not send here either merchants or wares, because it is our will that in these kingdoms there should not be any trade of slaves nor outlet for them.

*Letters from King Affonso of Kongo to the King of Portugal, 1526*

*A European account*

I remember that in the year 1681 an English trader got three hundred good slaves almost for nothing besides the trouble of receiving them at the beach in his boats, as the local men brought them from the field of battle, having obtained a victory over a neighbouring nation, and taken a great number of prisoners.

At other times slaves are so scarce there, that in 1682 I could get but eight from one end of the coast to the other, not only because we were a great number of trading ships on the coast at the same time, but by reason the natives were everywhere at peace . . .

As to the different sorts of goods the Europeans generally carry thither for trade; each nation commonly supplies the coast with such goods as their respective countries can afford; and what they want at home for well assorting their cargo, they buy in other parts of Europe.

*Jean Barbot, a French trader*

# 9 Merchant sailors on the east coast

*The statue of Bartolomeo Dias in Cape Town*

Meanwhile, the Portuguese had been trying to find their way round the southern cape to India. It was known that they would be able to buy spices there, which were nearly as valuable as the gold they were seeking in West Africa. These spices were ginger, cinnamon, pepper and nutmeg, which improved the taste of food. In Europe people killed their cattle at the end of the summer and kept the meat salted all through the winter. To improve the flavour of the meat, rich people paid a lot of money for spices.

Formerly traders had gone from Europe to India by land. Later, however, the Ottoman Turks had built a new Moslem Empire that stretched from North Africa to Persia. Christian traders were not allowed to pass through. The Portuguese, however, believed they could reach India by sea.

In 1487 Bartolomeo Dias sailed past the Cape of Good Hope, but his men were frightened by violent storms, and he had to turn back. Ten years later, however, Vasco da Gama, another Portuguese captain, tried again with three ships. This time the Portuguese continued round the Cape and then east and north along the coast.

## The Portuguese reach Mozambique

One day in March 1498 the Swahili of Mozambique were going about their morning business when a shout was heard. A man came running up from the harbour to warn the guards that three strange ships were approaching from beyond the reef. They carried more sails than Arab dhows, so the Swahili thought they must be Turkish ships. When the ships reached the harbour the visitors were welcomed and given food.

Soon, however, it was discovered that the strangers were Christians from Portugal. The Moslems of Mozambique knew that the Kalifs had been fighting wars against the Christians of Europe for a long time. The people of Mozambique therefore drove the Portuguese away.

Vasco da Gama was both surprised to find such a large town on the African coast and disappointed to be treated in this way. His voyage round the Cape had taken six months. He needed fresh food and water, and also hoped to find a pilot to show him the way across the sea to India.

*Mombasa from the anchorage a hundred years ago*

## They reach Mombasa and Malindi

*Vasco da Gama*

The Portuguese therefore sailed away northward along the coast. They did not stop at Kilwa, but they could see it in the distance and were again amazed at the appearance of a large town with mosques and streets and many houses. A similar view awaited them at Mombasa, and here they decided to land.

In the meantime, however, some Swahili sailed in a fast dhow from Mozambique to tell the people of Mombasa that the strangers were Christians, and that there had been a fight. When the Sultan of Mombasa heard this, he planned to trick Vasco da Gama by being friendly. When the ships had entered the harbour, he would sink them and kill the Portuguese.

Vasco da Gama waited outside the harbour, feeling suspicious of the Arabs. They brought him presents, but he still would not enter the harbour. Next day some Swahili came in boats and tried to cut the ropes holding the ships to anchor. The Portuguese captured two of them, and made them tell of the Sultan's plans. The news made Vasco da Gama decide not to find a pilot in Mombasa. He sailed on to Malindi instead.

The people of Malindi were rivals of the people of Mombasa. The Portuguese had discovered this, and thought the Sultan of Malindi would help them. They soon found they were right. The Sultan sent a present of six sheep, and promised to find a pilot. From that time the Portuguese and the people of Malindi were friends and allies.

**The Portuguese in India**

With the April monsoon wind blowing hard on their sails, the Portuguese crossed the sea to India, and came to Calicut.

The ruler of Calicut was very rich—much richer than the Portuguese. He even laughed at the presents Vasco da Gama had brought, but the Portuguese captain promised to come again with better presents. The Indians gave him spices of all kinds, together with silk from China, cotton cloth from India, and precious stones from Burma and Ceylon.

Then Vasco da Gama and his ships sailed for home: they had been away for three years. The King of Portugal and all the people gave them a great welcome. The king listened with great interest to all the stories they had to tell. He was amazed to hear about all the rich towns along the east coast of Africa.

**The Portuguese seize East Africa**

After this, the Portuguese sent ships year after year to India. They built forts at Ormuz in the Persian Gulf, at Goa in India, and at places in the East Indies. Portugal became wealthy and strong.

To make the journey safely, the Portuguese ships had to stop on the East African coast. They needed to mend the sails, and to take in fresh water and vegetables for the crew. But many Arab towns disliked the Portuguese and refused to help them. Of course, the Arabs were Moslem and the Portuguese were Christian, but the main reason was that the Arabs wanted the trade in the Indian Ocean all for themselves. Being determined to take this trade away from them, the Portuguese decided to conquer the East African towns.

Between 1502 and 1507, the Portuguese captured most of the towns. They were able to do this because they were determined fighters, and because they had better guns than the Arabs.

First, the Portuguese went to Kilwa and told the Sultan to pay tribute. He refused, so the Portuguese sent soldiers into the town and occupied it. Later they built Kilwa Castle, which is still standing today. After occupying Kilwa, they attacked Mombasa. This was more difficult. There was a hard fight in the narrow streets and on the rooftops. In the end the Portuguese won, after many houses had been destroyed.

In the north, the Portuguese made Malindi their chief town. The Sultan of Malindi was a friend, and did not have to pay tribute like other sultans. Later a fort was built at Mombasa,

*Memorial pillar erected to Vasco da Gama at Malindi: an early 19th century drawing*

and the Portuguese officer at Malindi was called 'Captain of the coast of Malindi and the Fort of Mombasa'. Farther north still the Portuguese visited Ethiopia, and in 1540 they helped the Christian king of Ethiopia to defeat the Moslem invaders (see Chapter 11, Book One).

In the south, the chief town of the Portuguese was at Mozambique. There too the Sultan was friendly. The Portuguese built a fort and a hospital, and the church of St Gabriel. All these were built of stone. Around the town the Portuguese planted fruit trees and vegetable gardens, so that sailors on their way to India could have fresh food. In this way, new crops and fruits, such as maize, groundnuts and pawpaw, came to East Africa.

The Captain at Mozambique controlled Sofala and the gold trade, which the Portuguese were now taking from the Arabs.

## The Portuguese in Mashonaland

As we know, the Portuguese had come to East Africa because it was on the way to India and the spice trade.

Soon after their arrival, however, they heard about the gold trade at Sofala (see Chapters 12 and 13, Book One). Gold was even more valuable than spices. Adventurers from Spain, a country next to Portugal, were discovering gold in South America. The Portuguese had found some in West Africa, but not enough. If they could find gold in East Africa they would be as rich and powerful as Spain, their great rival.

The Portuguese decided to find out where the gold at Sofala came from. In 1512, Antonio Fernandes with some African porters was sent into Mashonaland through the Sabi valley. Fernandes was an educated man who had offended the King of Portugal. To win a pardon, he had to perform some dangerous service. This journey was that service.

Fernandes reached Monomotapa's capital at Fura Mountain, and was given a friendly greeting by the Shona. On his return he reported that there was much gold, especially in Manicaland. The people were digging for it, sometimes fifty feet deep under the ground. In other places gold was washed from the streams. Nuggets as big as a man's fingernail were to be found. The climate, according to Fernandes, was good for Europeans to live in.

## Gonzales da Silveira

Many years passed. The Portuguese were busy winning the coast from the Arabs as far north as Malindi.

At last in 1561 a Jesuit missionary arrived in Mashonaland. He was Gonzales da Silveira, and he had come from Goa in India. He had heard of Monomotapa and wanted to convert him to Christianity.

The Monomotapa at this time was Nogoma Mapunzagatu, a young boy who was still being helped by his mother. He welcomed da Silveira with gifts of gold, cattle and slaves, but the priest declined them, saying he only wanted to win the hearts and minds of the people. At once he began teaching and baptizing.

The Arabs at Fura Mountain were angry. They feared that the Portuguese would now come and take all their trade. They told Nogoma that Silveira was using bad magic in order to destroy the kingdom. The young king was frightened, and decided to kill the missionary. Silveira was strangled in the night, and his body was thrown into the river, together with the bodies of several newly-baptized people.

When this news reached Portugal, more missionaries were sent. They continued working in Mashonaland for a hundred years, but their influence disappeared when the Portuguese were finally driven away.

## Trade in Mashonaland

The first Portuguese trading expedition came to Mashonaland in 1569. This time, in spite of the Arabs, Monomotapa agreed that the Europeans could dig for gold and silver, or buy it from the Africans, in certain places. In return, they had to pay a tax in cloth, and also help Monomotapa in war against enemy tribes.

The Portuguese now built trading posts at Masapa on the Upper Mazoe River and at two other places. All their trade going into and out of the country had to pass through these posts. True to their promise, they helped Monomotapa Gatsi Rusere (1596–1627) in his wars. After this, a new treaty was made, by which the white men were allowed to sit in the presence of the king, and did not have to bow low and clap their hands.

## The Shona drive out the Portuguese

The Shona, however, resented the growing influence of the Portuguese. In 1629 Monomotapa Kapararidze joined with the Arabs and made war on the white men. A great battle at Fura Mountain was won by the Portuguese and their allies. Kapararidze was killed and his place was taken by Mavura, a nephew, who had Portuguese support.

For a time all was peaceful again, and trade revived. However, the Arabs continued to make trouble, and the Portuguese were always insecure. Finally, in 1693, the Shona made another great effort. We have read in Chapter 12, Book One, how Monomotapa made an alliance with Changamire in the south, and how the Portuguese were finally driven from the country.

This was really a disaster for the Shona as well as for the Portuguese, because it meant less trade. There was no hope of a Portuguese revival, however, for they were also struggling without success against other enemies on the coast. The most important of these were the Arabs.

## The Portuguese at Mombasa

From the beginning, the Arabs had hated the Portuguese for taking away their trade, and for winning control of the Indian Ocean. The people of Mombasa especially made trouble. In 1588 the Turks were fighting a war against Portugal and Spain in the Mediterranean. They heard of the quarrel between Mombasa and the Portuguese, and sent a fleet to help the people of Mombasa. A rebellion started.

Ships and soldiers were sent from Goa to punish the people of Mombasa and to defeat the Turks. This might have been difficult, because the Turks were brave fighters with good weapons. But just at this time a fierce group of Bantu warriors called waZimba appeared on the mainland. The Zimba were not a proper tribe and we do not know where they came from. They were terrible savages and used to eat the flesh of their victims.

The Zimba rushed across the shallow water to the island of Mombasa, and killed everyone they could find. Many Arabs, Swahili and Turks were killed, as well as some Portuguese. After feasting and dancing, the Zimba left Mombasa, and the Portuguese who had come from Goa occupied it again.

After leaving Mombasa, some of the Zimba went north to Malindi, but there they were defeated by a brave Bantu tribe called waSegeju. Many Zimba were killed. The rest of the Zimba retreated southward, slaughtering people wherever they went. When they came to the Zambezi valley, they attacked and killed the Africans and Portuguese there. After that, the Zimba passed on and disappeared.

## Fort Jesus

At Mombasa, the Portuguese then built a great stone fort which they called Fort Jesus. It was started in 1592. It had high walls and a great courtyard inside. At each corner was a tower from which defenders could fire at attackers. Around the outside a deep ditch was dug. The front of the fort looked out over the sea.

For a hundred years, Portuguese soldiers lived in the fort with their wives and families. They put down rebellions in Mombasa, and kept the Portuguese strong in other parts of the coast.

During this time, from about 1600 to 1700, the enemies of Portugal grew stronger. Other countries in Europe fought against Portugal, and started to send ships to India. The Arabs in Arabia saw this happen, and began to fight to win back the East African towns. In the interior the Bantu tribes and the

*Fort Jesus, built by the Portuguese in 1593*

Nilo-Hamites were increasing in numbers, and kept making war on the Portuguese.

At last even Fort Jesus was not strong enough to protect them.

**Omani Arabs**

There was a great ruler of Oman in Arabia, whose name was Seif bin Sultan. In 1696 he sent seven ships to attack Mombasa. The town was captured, and the Arabs besieged Fort Jesus.

In the fort were about two thousand five hundred people, of whom about a hundred were Portuguese. Months passed, and there was not enough food for so many. Then there came a terrible sickness, and hundreds died. After nearly three years, there were only twenty people left alive in the fort. They surrendered to the Arabs.

This was the end of Portuguese rule on the north part of the coast. Without Fort Jesus they could not control the other towns. The new rulers from Oman often treated the people very badly. Sometimes the Portuguese were asked for help, but they were not strong enough. They were only able to hold on to Mozambique, and their trading posts in the Zambezi valley.

In the next chapter we shall read more of what had been happening in the interior of East Africa, and how east coast trade was just beginning to affect the lives of people inland.

# 10 Peoples and kingdoms of East Africa

El Masoudi, the Arabian traveller, had reported that black-skinned people—'the people of Zanj'— were living on the east coast by the time of his visit in 916. These people were the first wave of Bantu-speaking settlers who had arrived in that part of Africa during the previous two or three centuries. They must have been the ancestors of coast tribes such as the Taita and the Nyika in Kenya, the Shambaa and the Zaramo along the Zanzibar coast, and the Ngindo and the Makwa farther south towards the Rovuma River. During the next few hundred years, more Bantu-speaking people continued to find their way to East Africa from the region of the Congo Highlands.

Now we come to a new series of movements. These are very important, and to understand them you must look carefully at the map. They begin with an event in the north-east about A.D. 1300.

## The Galla

Some time about 1300, a new Hamitic people arrived in Somaliland from South Arabia. These were the Galla. They were a tall, brown-skinned, straight-nosed people who herded cattle. They had the custom of age-sets, which meant that all boys born in the same year grew up together, trained together, and fought together in war. This custom later spread to many of the Bantu tribes of Kenya.

First, the Galla went south-west to the country which is now north-east Kenya. Then they moved north. By about 1450 they were north of Lake Rudolf. During their migration, they met some early Hamites and Stone Age hunters; but these were few and there was room for the Galla. It was not until the Galla met the Sidama Hamites north of Lake Rudolf that they stopped.

The Galla and the Sidama were both cattle-keeping Hamitic tribes, but they were fighting tribes and there were wars between them for grazing lands. Many Sidama Hamites were pushed out of their homes to the west, towards the Upper Nile.

## Hima and Tutsi

After reaching the Nile, some of these Sidama moved south with their long-horned cattle, through the lake region, till they came to Ruanda and Burundi north of Lake Tanganyika. Here

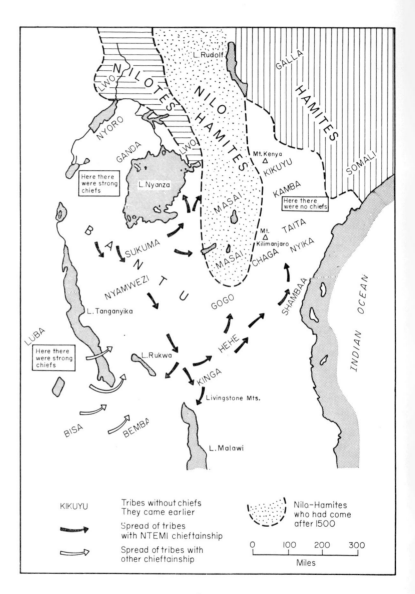

*The spread of chieftainship from the lake region to East Africa about 1700–1800*

KIKUYU — Tribes without chiefs
They came earlier

→ Spread of tribes with NTEMI chieftainship

⇨ Spread of tribes with other chieftainship

⋯ Nilo-Hamites who had come after 1500

0   100   200   300
Miles

they conquered the Bantu, who were Iru and Hutu. The traditions of these Bantu tell of how they were conquered long ago by a tall and able people, a race of heroes whom they called the Chwezi. We believe that these people were the Sidama from the north. Their descendants today are called Hima in the north, that is, in southern Uganda and Ruanda, and are known as Tutsi in the south, that is, in Burundi.

The Chwezi chiefs did not mix very much with the early Bantu, but kept to themselves the special task of ruling. This separation of the ruling class in Ruanda-Burundi has continued until recent times. They became strong and able rulers. However, at this time, if not before, they became a Bantu-speaking people.

Many of the customs of Uganda and Ruanda-Burundi have come from the Chwezi, the ancestors of the Hima and Tutsi. Much ceremonial attended the life of the chief, or king. These kings lived in large palaces built in a cone-shape, rather like the palace in which the Kabaka of Bugunda lived until the revolution of 1966. Wooden drinking vessels now came to be used, an old Sidama custom. The Chwezi taught their subjects how to make bark cloth, how to cultivate coffee, and how to dig wells through rock, using iron picks. They brought in new kinds of spear and shield.

The Chwezi ruled most of the lake region in peace for about two hundred years until the Lwo invasion of about 1600, about which we shall read later in this chapter.

## Nilo-Hamites: the Masai

Meanwhile, others of the Sidama Hamites, who were pushed out of their homes by the Galla and went towards the Nile, mixed with the Nilotic peoples who lived there. In this way, they formed a new people whom we call the *Nilo-Hamites*. This change happened about 1400–1450.

A hundred years later, these Nilo-Hamites were moving southward, along Lake Rudolf and into the great Rift Valley. Later they split into two main tribes, the Masai and the Nandi. You will read mostly about the Masai. Other tribes were the Turkana and the Suk.

The Masai, like the Sidama, had come from a very dry country. For many months there was little grass for the cattle, and rain was very important. In a drought the cattle would die, and then the people would die. Because of this, the most important people among the Masai were the rain-makers, or priests who prayed for rain. The leading rain-maker was called the *Laibon*, and he acted as chief of the tribe.

According to their stories, the early Masai were led up from Lake Rudolf in the Rift Valley to the Uasin Gishu Plateau in

Kenya by a founder-chief called Maasinda. They say that Maasinda built a great ladder for the climb. From here they moved southward along the line of the Rift Valley, looking for better grazing lands. By 1600 they were living as far south as Kilimanjaro and northern Tanzania.

Most of this area was open highland country. It was good for hunting and herding cattle, but not for farming. That was why it had been left empty by the early Bantu tribes who came to East Africa before the Masai. Now the Masai were a fighting people. They were iron workers, and had great iron spears. The head of a spear was three feet long. It was sharp and heavy and could pierce any shield or even kill a buffalo. The Masai had an old story that God had given them their cattle, and that all cattle belonged to their tribe. They fought all the people round about for their herds, and would cheerfully go three hundred miles for a raid. They were invincible in the open. With their regiments of spearmen, with their long shields and their plumes waving in the sun, they terrified all who met them. But they could not conquer people who lived in wooded country and fought with bows and arrows. They remained in the open savannas, raiding from their headquarters near Lake Naivasha, proud and scornful of all other men.

*Masai tribesmen*

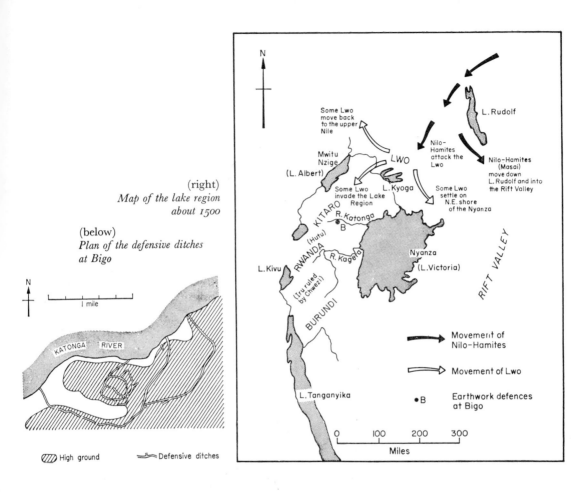

(right)
*Map of the lake region about 1500*

(below)
*Plan of the defensive ditches at Bigo*

N

|——————| 1 mile

KATONGA RIVER

▨ High ground    Defensive ditches

## The southern Nilotes: the Lwo

Some of the Nilo-Hamites, such as the Lango, the Teso and the Karamojong, instead of going south like the Masai, moved south-west towards Lake Kyoga. Here they met the Lwo-speaking Nilotes, who had moved south up the Nile from the Nilotic homeland.

The Nilo-Hamites drove out the Lwo. Some Lwo moved south to the shore of Lake Nyanza, where they live today in the Lake Province of Kenya. Others turned back to the north-west, where they are still living, in the Sudan. Still others moved into the lake region, into the part which is present-day Uganda. Here lived the early Bantu, many of whom were being ruled by the Chwezi chiefs, also known as the Hima.

These Lwo came south. They appeared to the Bantu as a strange and terrible people. Tall and dark-skinned, they were said to be as many as the grains of millet in a good harvest. Their spears were of iron—even the haft of a spear was sometimes made of iron. Nothing could stop them, and they advanced south to the Katonga River, the boundary of the Chwezi kingdom of Ruanda.

Here the Chwezi made a great effort to stop the Lwo. They built earthwork defences along the river. The biggest, with earth mounds and trenches a mile long, some dug out of the rock, was at Bigo. It guarded the most important ford on the middle Katonga. Even this did not stop the Lwo armies, however, and the Chwezi-Hutu people had to escape south into the Ruanda of today.

## Bunyoro

The Lwo settled down in the north, and there founded the kingdom of Bunyoro. The Lwo chiefs of Bunyoro were of the Bito clan. Most of the Lwo soon married Bantu wives, however, and Bunyoro became a Bantu kingdom. Their kings had the title of Mukama.

The heart of Bunyoro lay south of the Kafu River, from Singo across to northern Toro. Around this country, the Nyoro set up subject kingdoms, and gave them chiefs of the Bito clan. They took many of the customs of the Chwezi, which they learned from their new subjects. Some of the new provinces were Buddu, Kyaka, Bungungu and Buruli. Later the Nyoro extended their power to Ankole in the south, to the Toro north of Ruwenzori, and to Busoga on the border of present-day Kenya. By 1600 they were the strongest empire in East Africa.

## Buganda

On the north-west shore of Lake Nyanza lived a small Bantu tribe called the Ganda. They had had a legendary founder chief called Kintu, but by this time they were ruled by Bito chiefs whom they called Kabaka.

None the less, Buganda was not really part of the Nyoro Empire. In 1600 the Nyoro tried to conquer them, but they were beaten off in a great battle at Mbale. The Ganda were helped by the fishermen of the Sese Islands in the lake, and they always remembered this alliance with gratitude. The Nyoro left the Ganda and turned to fight in the south.

Then, about 1650, there began a great change. The Nyoro

crossed the Kagera River beyond Ankole, and invaded Karagwe. But here they were far from home, and their great army was defeated.

When the news reached Buganda, the people called for revenge on Bunyoro for past raids. Kabaka Katerega, the eleventh Ganda king, led his armies north and west, and soon doubled the size of the Ganda kingdom. After this, from 1700 to 1800, Buganda continued to grow. On the map you can see how this happened.

During this time, the Kabakas became stronger rulers. They began to live in grass-and-reed palaces in the Chwezi style. Two very harsh rulers were Kagulu and Kikulwe, but although they were hated by the people, they strengthened the kabakaship. Then the next step was to put an end to the system of

*The growth of Buganda*
*1600–1800*

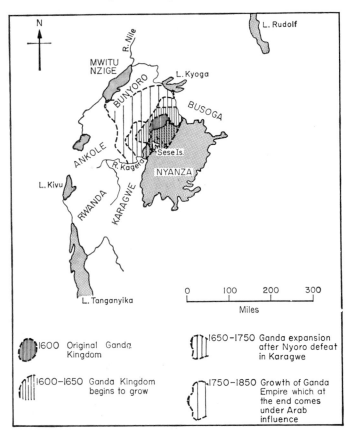

allowing the provinces to be ruled by hereditary chiefs. This reform began when Kabaka Junju took the great province of Buddu from Bunyoro in about 1750. Buddu was given an appointed governor, who was no more than a civil servant. The same thing was done in other provinces. It gave the Kabaka more control in his country.

By 1800, Buganda was the strongest kingdom in the lake region. It controlled the whole western shore of Lake Nyanza from the Kagera to the Nile. Bunyoro was now only a small kingdom to the north-east.

The growth of Buganda was also helped by trade. Junju's successor, Kabaka Semakokiro, opened a long-distance trade with the Nyamwezi south of Lake Nyanza. The Nyamwezi, about whom you will read later in this chapter, already traded with the Arabs on the coast. The most important part of this trade was the export of ivory. The Ganda raided Bunyoro and beyond for ivory, and in the nineteenth century for slaves. After 1850, as you will read in Chapter 13, Arabs themselves came to Buganda. In this way, because they commanded the entrance to the lake region from the south-east, the Ganda were able to become a wealthy as well as a powerful people.

**Tanzania**

Away to the south-east of the lake region lies the wide land which today we call Tanzania. Most of it is a dry, wide plain with some ranges of hills in the south. Only one important river flows through it, the Rufiji. There are no marked natural features that would encourage a tribe to form a kingdom with firm frontiers, and the land was too poor for the people to farm easily. Perhaps that is why early Bantu tribes like the early Sotho and the Karanga passed straight through the country on their way south to look for better land. However, there were many herds of wild game and thousands of elephant. Tanganyika became one of the biggest sources of ivory in Africa.

After A.D. 1000 the country was inhabited by small tribes of early Bantu. Most of them had come from the Congo region. There were also a few Bushmen and early Hamites, but these were steadily driven out or absorbed by the new Iron Age peoples.

These small Bantu-speaking tribes did not have chiefs at first. They lived in small clans loosely joined together in groups. But you may remember that the early Bantu of the lake region,

*Elephants in Tanzanian landscape*

who had come from the Sudan, did have chiefs, even in the days before the Hima invasion. Now the Tanganyikan tribes nearest to Lake Nyanza began to adopt the idea of chiefs from the peoples of the lake region.

**'Ntemi' chieftainship**

This change took place because a tribe led by a chief was stronger and better organized than one without a chief. Strong groups looking for better land were able to overcome the villages to the south, and the leader would set himself up as ruler. All western Tanganyikan tribes say that their chieftainships were begun by cattle-owning strangers from the northwest. Moreover, all of them call their chiefs by the title of *Ntemi*. *Ntemi* comes from a word meaning 'to cut'—perhaps because the chief was the person who cut short discussion and came to a decision; perhaps because he was the man of the axe, a symbol of chieftainship.

In fact the Ntemi was a sort of 'divine king'. He controlled the sacred fire of the tribe, which must not go out. He controlled the forge, and the men who smelted iron for the tribe.

When he fell ill, his death was hastened, and he was buried in a special way with his servants, who were also sacrificed.

The spread of Ntemi chieftainship from north to south through western Tanganyika probably happened between about 1200 and 1500.

## Unyamwezi

Most of the Ntemi kingdoms were quite small. Some had only about a thousand subjects. The largest was the kingdom of the Nyamwezi, with their allies, the Sukuma. These people lived south of Lake Nyanza and east of Burundi. They followed the custom that the son inherits from the father. They kept cattle, but these were different from the long-horned Hima cattle.

*Shore of Lake Nyanza*

From this we know that their rulers came from the lake region before the Hima conquest.

First they extended their power southward to the Iringa highlands, where the Hehe people lived. Next, the Sukuma dominated the country east of Lake Nyanza, until then the home of pastoralists and hunters. Finally in the eighteenth century the Nyamwezi began to control Gogo country in the east.

Because of this, many tribes beyond Nyamwezi country came to be ruled by Ntemi chiefs, although they were not part of the Nyamwezi kingdom. Among these tribes were the Namwanga and the Nyakyusa in the south, the Kinga, the Bena and the Hehe in the south-east, and the Gogo in the east. Farther east still, even the Sagara and the Shambaa, only a hundred miles from the coast, began to have Ntemi chiefs by about 1750. To the north-east, of course, this influence was stopped by the presence of the warrior Nilo-Hamites such as the Masai.

## Ivory trade

In time the Nyamwezi became a great trading people. By 1750 they had learned that the Swahili and Arabs of the coast would pay well in cloth for ivory.

The ivory trade needed organized rule: elephants had to be hunted, and all the tusks brought in; carriers had to be recruited and sent in large parties to the coast; and armed guards had to go with the trading parties to protect them. The Nyamwezi, being the largest kingdom not too far from the coastal markets, became the ivory traders of East Africa. After 1800, large parties with hundreds of men made the long, hot march from Unyamwezi to the sea.

Nyamwezi men became known as the finest carriers in East Africa. Nyamwezi children used to start practising with small tusks on their heads from an early age.

## Kenya

We now come to the remaining part of East Africa. This is present-day Kenya, between the highlands and the sea. Most of the present Bantu inhabitants arrived about 1600 from Tanganyika to the south. They settled in the well-wooded country around Mount Kenya. The most important tribes were the Kikuyu and the Kamba inland, and the Taita and the Nyika near the sea.

These tribes remained without chiefs until recent times.

They were too far north for the Ntemi system to reach them. Their country was isolated from the rest of Bantu Africa. To the north was the dry country where the nomadic Somali and Galla lived. To the west were the warrior Masai in the highlands above the Rift Valley, and to the east was the sea. South, from where they had come, was Mount Kilimanjaro, and beyond it the dry coastal plain.

## The Kikuyu

When the Kikuyu first arrived in this country, they found already living there an early Bantu tribe called Ndorobo. These Ndorobo were a primitive people who used stone as well as iron. They made pit-dwellings covered with roofs of wild banana leaves, and lived by hunting in the forest. They buried their dead carefully, and worshipped the ancestral spirits.

The Kikuyu, who were cattle farmers at first, lived in more open country, and were friendly towards the Ndorobo. In alliance with them, and even with the Masai, they fought a Galla invasion from the north and drove them out. The Kikuyu

*Early photograph of an elephant hunt*

*A Kikuyu village*

have a story that before the war their leaders asked the advice of Supi, a famous medicine-man. Supi told the Ndorobo to bring sandals made of leather with hair on both sides; the Masai had to bring a bull whose dung was white; while the Kikuyu were instructed to find a rare mole called a *huko*. The Ndorobo made their sandals from the ears of a donkey; the Masai brought a bull fed only on milk; and the Kikuyu found their mole. They then went into battle, each tribe with its special charm, and won the war.

However, the Masai now turned on the Kikuyu and began to capture their herds. The Kikuyu retreated to the forests, and began to clear them in order to cultivate grain crops. The Ndorobo, who lived in the forest, were now driven out to the north, and their numbers decreased. The Masai repeatedly attacked the Kikuyu, but the Kikuyu, armed with bows and arrows, fought them from the forest and drove them back. By 1800 they were the strongest tribe around Mount Kenya, and worshipped a god called Ngai who, they said, lived in the mountain.

*Mount Kenya*

## The Kamba

South-east of Mount Kenya lived the Kamba. Like the Nyamwezi inland, they were a trading people. To the Arabs on the coast they sold ivory and cattle. From them they bought cotton, glass beads, copper wire and salt. They sold these goods from the coast to the Kikuyu for food. Kamba country was dry, and famine frequent.

## Engaruka

Before leaving this chapter on the peoples of East Africa, you should read about one mystery that has puzzled historians. This mystery is the remains of a town at Engaruka, twenty miles south of Lake Natron in the Rift Valley. Terraces cover the hill-slopes, and on them are the remains of over six thousand rough stone houses. The town was destroyed about three hundred years ago, probably by the Masai, and its inhabitants driven out. Who were they? Of what race and language? Perhaps one day we shall know. Today we believe that Engaruka was built by the early Hamites who lived in East Africa before the Bantu came (see Chapter 10, Book One).

**An account of *Ntemi* chieftainship**

Turi set out with the men of Vuga, a very great army, young men and elders, with two war-horns and his flute and his signal-horn. . . .

And they came to that place with song and dance, and every man vaunted his prowess and glorified his country and boasted of his pre-eminence and rank.

And Turi, their headman, was received with shouts of applause. And he proclaimed his skill in his craft, and glorified the fire of his forge, and boasted how he slew the men of Pare with his spear, and how he beat out arrows and axes and hammers and knives. . . . And he boasted that he was rich in oxen and goats and sheep, and he claimed that it was he who protected all the people and cared for them with gentle kindness. And at every word he asked his people, 'Is this that I say true or false?' and his people responded with one voice, 'It is true.'

. . . .

Whoever comes to this country of Usambara must admit that he is Turi's man. That clan holds the country because God gave them the gift of working iron, and skill in war. . . . None but they have ornaments, none dares to boast himself a son of the country.

from the *Habari za Wakilindi*

# East African Time Chart

| Date | The Lake Region | Kenya and Tanzania | East Coast |
|---|---|---|---|
| A.D. | Possibly some early Hamitic Stone Age inhabitants. | Interior inhabited by small groups of brown-skinned early Hamites of Stone Age culture. | Some Indian traders visit east coast. |
| 100 | | | *Periplus of Erythrean Sea* written by Greek trader. |
| 200 | | | |
| 300 | | | |
| 400 | | | Rhapta and other 'Azanian' coastal towns flourishing on Arabian and Indian trade. |
| 500 | | | |
| 600 | | | The *Hijra* of Mohammed. |
| 700 | Some early Bantu settlers had probably arrived by this time. | Early Iron Age Bantu begin to arrive from the Congo region. | Arab and Persian settlements begin as far south as Kilwa. |
| 800 | | | Decline of Rhapta and other African coast towns. |
| 900 | | | |
| 1000 | | | El Masoudi makes first report of black people living on the east coast. Kilwa grows into a large town. |
| 1100 | | | Kilwa gains control of Sofala. |
| 1200 | | | 'Golden Age' of Kilwa begins. |
| 1300 | | Spread of *Ntemi* chieftainship from Karagwe begins. Galla migration through Somaliland and northern Kenya begins. | |
| 1400 | | | Kilwa begins to decline. |
| 1500 | Galla meet Sidama north of Lake Rudolf. Results: 1. Chwezi conquest of lake region. 2. Nilo-Hamites formed. 3. Lwo invasion of lake region. Kingdom of Bunyoro established. Nyoro defeated in Karagwe. Kabaka Katerega leads Ganda. | Early Hamitic town of Engaruka flourishing. Nilo-Hamites (e.g. Masai) move south, destroying Engaruka. Chiefless tribes (e.g. Kikuyu) move into N.E. Kenya. Wars with Galla and Masai. | Rise of Pate. Sofala becomes independent. Portuguese arrive on east coast. Kilwa and other towns captured. Fort Jesus built at Mombasa. |
| 1600 | | | |
| 1700 | | | Seif bin Sultan attacks Mombasa, takes Fort Jesus. Portuguese driven from east coast north of Mozambique. |
| 1800 | Growth of Buganda. Buganda the strongest kingdom in the lake region. Trade with Arabs develops. | Nyamwezi begin trading between lake region and the coast. Ngoni groups conquer tribes in S. Tanzania. | Sayyid Said, Sultan of Oman, comes to Zanzibar. |
| 1900 | | Arab traders move inland. | Rapid growth of slave trade. |

# 11 Bantu from the Congo highlands

Let us now look back and consider the movement of the Bantu peoples as a whole.

The homeland, or what is sometimes called the cradleland, of the Bantu-speaking peoples had been the western Sudan, towards what is today the Cameroons. After learning about the manufacture and use of iron, the Bantu-speaking peoples moved south. They moved, you may remember, along two main routes.

First were the cattle-owning tribes. These tribes mostly had chiefs, and generally followed the custom of the son inheriting from the father. They had first travelled east across the Sudan, and then south, entering the lake region. Some early tribes, such as the Karanga, Sotho, Abenguni and Venda, went even farther south, past the lakes, beyond the Zambezi and even to South Africa. Other later tribes such as the Iru, the Hutu and the Ganda settled down in the lake region.

Next we noticed the early Bantu of Tanganyika. These tribes followed the custom of the son inheriting from the father, but they did not keep cattle, and at first they did not have chiefs. These early tribes came, not from the lake region to the north, but from the Congo in the west.

**Other tribes from the Congo**

We shall now read about other tribes which came to south-east Africa from the Congo in the west. These Bantu-speaking people had also come from the western Sudan long ago, but their route of migration had been along the Upper Congo basin. In the west and centre of the Congo basin there is dense forest, but these tribes kept to the eastern highlands as much as possible. At last they passed south of Lake Tanganyika and moved east across the Lualaba. They came in the end to north-eastern Zambia and Lake Malawi.

Most of these tribes did not keep cattle. They followed the custom that the son inherits from the mother, and goes to live at his wife's village. Generally they had chiefs.

**Malawi**

The Malawi are those tribes which settled along the east and south of Lake Malawi, and in between the Luangwa and Zambezi Rivers, before the Abenguni came. At first they were one

*Fishing canoes on the shore
of Lake Malawi*

tribe, divided into clans. The chiefs of the three largest clans
were called Karonga, Undi and Mwase. Their old stories say that
at one time they lived near the Luba tribe of the Upper Congo.
They reached the north of Lake Malawi some time after 1400.

Some of the Malawi settled down at the north end of Lake
Malawi under Karonga. They liked the fertile valleys where
crops grew well. There was plenty of rain because wind from
the far-off ocean blew over the mountains. Iron was to be
found in the district. Later they learned fishing from the earliest
Bantu inhabitants, such as the Nkonde, the Henga and the
Tumbuka.

Most of the Malawi moved farther south to the country west
of the Shire River. By this time they had lived long enough
near Lake Malawi to call themselves the 'Lake People', which
in their language is *Mang'anja*. Their chiefs were called Mkanda.
They lived peacefully in their neat villages, cultivating their
fields of millet and banana, looking after their flocks of sheep
and goats, and making their excellent iron-work.

## Cewa kingdoms

About 1500 the Mang'anja were increasing in numbers, and
some clans moved away to the west. These clans called themselves Cewa, although they were still of the Malawi tribe and
spoke nearly the same language.

First, there were the Cewa led by Mwase. They went up to
the uninhabited Luangwa valley. They made the chief's village
at Kasungu, and still live in that district today. Other Malawi
calling themselves Cewa moved farther west and settled down at

Petauke. They also hunted and farmed and lived peacefully.

Beyond the Luangwa lived some early Bantu who had come from Katanga country a long time before. The Cewa mixed peacefully with these people, and formed a new tribe living beside their own, called the Nsenga. The Nsenga chiefs were named Kalindawalu.

There were many elephants in Malawi country. Because of this, the Arabs and Portuguese came to trade there later on. When they came for ivory they also took away people captive. That is why the Malawi suffered badly from the slave trade, but this did not happen until after 1800.

**Bemba**

After the Malawi, another people came from the southern Congo to the north-east Zambian plateau. These were the Bemba. The Bemba did not go as far as Lake Malawi, but stayed west of the Luangwa River.

The Bemba homeland, which they call *Kola*, was in northern Angola. The Kasai River runs from there into the Congo, but the Bemba stayed on the plateau. They were not a river people. They spoke a Luba language, and did not keep cattle. They followed the custom of the son inheriting from the mother.

The Bemba had chiefs from early times. These chiefs were strong and sometimes harsh rulers. The founder chief, who was called Nshinga, may have lived about 1500. A later chief called Kapopo was an unpopular ruler, and some of the tribe fled away to settle on the Lualaba. Here developed the Bemba tribe as we know it.

The Bemba conquered the valley people and learned to speak their language, which is Cibemba today. From this time, their chiefs took the title *Mukulu* or *Mukulumpe*, which means 'The Great One'.

About 1670, their chief was Mulopwe. He tried to make the people work hard, cutting grass in the dry season. The people became discontented, and his sons protested. Mulopwe threatened to kill one of his sons called Chiti. So Chiti with his brother Nkole led their clans away, south of Lake Mweru. Here they defeated the Shila in battle, and crossed the Luapula.

**Chitimukulu**

After the Bemba had crossed the Luapula, small clans broke away to find lands of their own. There was plenty of land, for the only people living in this region were Bushmen. Among the

Bemba clans which now made separate tribes were the Ushi, the Chishinga, the Bisa and the Senga. The Bisa went south of Lake Bangweulu. The Senga moved east, up to the Muchinga escarpment.

For a short time the main Bemba tribe went south-east into the Muchingas and tried to cross the Luangwa. Here they found the Nsenga and the Cewa under Mwase, who had arrived a hundred years before. The Bemba fought the Cewa and won this small war, but Chiti was killed.

Now Chiti's nephew, according to Bemba custom, became paramount chief, and took the title of Chitimukulu. He led the tribe north across the Chambeshi River, and finally settled on the plateau to the north. Here the Bemba became a powerful nation. They ruled the country between Lakes Bangweulu, Mweru and Tanganyika and the headwaters of the Luangwa River.

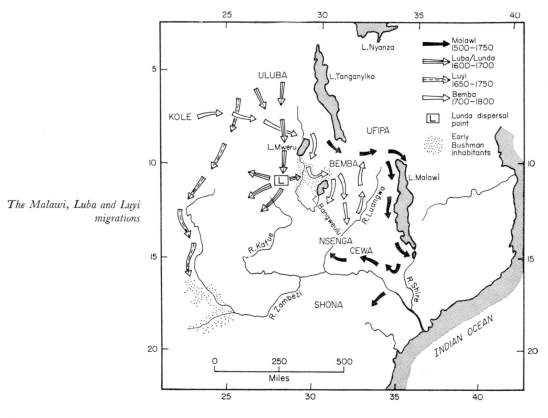

*The Malawi, Luba and Luyi migrations*

## The Lunda dispersal

Meanwhile, another great Bantu-speaking tribe had been growing powerful in the southern Congo. This was the Luba nation, about whom we read in Chapter 7. The Luba, like their cousins, the Bemba, had come south from the Cameroons to the Angola highlands where the Kasai begins. They had left the Cameroons later than other Bantu, and were possibly related to the great Yoruba nation, a Negro tribe in Nigeria (Chapter 6). Later the Luba moved away from Angola. By 1600 the Luba kingdom extended from the Lubilashi to the Lualaba River.

Before long an important new branch of the Luba was formed to the south. This was the Lunda, who have a story that Iala Mwaku was chief of a Luba clan called Bungu. About 1600, when Iala Mwaku was an old man, he was badly treated by his three sons. Iala therefore said that, when he died, the chieftainship must pass to his grand-daughter, a young princess named Lueji. For this purpose, he gave Lueji the *lukano* bracelet, the symbol of royal power.

Iala's sons were so angry that they took their clans away from Buluba. One of them, Chinguri, went as far as Luanda and met the Portuguese there in 1609. Another, Chinyama, went south-west and founded the Lovale tribe.

Meanwhile, Lueji had become queen, and married a Luba hunter named Chibinda Ilunga. She presented Chibinda with the *lukano* bracelet which gave him the chief's authority. At about this time the people of Lueji and Chibinda began to call themselves the Lunda tribe.

Chibinda's grandson, Iavo Naweji, extended the Lunda kingdom to the south. This high sandy plateau, the Congo-Zambezi watershed, was then empty of people. The Lunda clans which now settled there were led by Musokantanda, Kanongesha and Ishinde. The Lunda people were now a powerful empire with vast lands, and Iavo Naweji was given the title of 'lord of wealth', or *mwata yamvo*.

Although the country was not very good for farming, there were quantities of ivory. The Lunda also discovered new supplies of copper ore, which they called *katanga*. They became good copper workers. They made copper bracelets and ankle rings, and copper bars cross-shaped in section. Copper and ivory were sent to the west coast Portuguese, in exchange for cloth and beads.

*X-shaped copper bar*

## The Luapula Lunda

Some time after Iavo Naweji died, the Lunda attacked the Shila in the Luapula valley, and conquered them. This was about 1740. Bilonda, a grandson of Iavo, was made ruler of the Luapula settlement, and took the title of Kazembe.

Bilonda even went with an army across the north-eastern plateau as far as the Luangwa. But the Bemba clans were already settling there, and in any case the Lunda preferred the Luapula valley with its rich soil and its fish supplies.

Mwata Yamvo traded with Luanda. Kazembe did the same, but he also tried to open trade with the east coast. He had heard of the Arabs and the Portuguese there. In 1798 a Portuguese traveller, Dr Lacerda, came to his village from Tete, but he died of fever. The Bemba and Bisa were unfriendly to travellers. After 1850, however, Arab traders from Kilwa and Zanzibar came to live on the Luapula, and an ivory, copper and slave trade began.

## The Luyi

West of Luba country, yet another tribe, the Luyi, was moving south. *Baluyi* means 'river people', and the Luyi had for some time been living in the Kasai River valley.

The Luyi were separate from the Luba, but were related to them. An old story says that the two tribes had the same founder chief, who was a woman called Mbuywamwamba. The Luyi, like the Luba, did not keep cattle. Unlike them, they did not even have chiefs to begin with.

Coming south from the Kasai some time after 1500, the Luyi settled in the valley plain of the Upper Zambezi. Here they started to have chiefs, of whom the first was called Mboo. They also learned from the Ila on the Kafue plateau the practice of keeping cattle. With fish, cattle and the fertile land of the flood-plain, the Luyi became a wealthy and powerful nation. They subdued several of the surrounding tribes, and even fought the Lovale in the north.

Their greatest ruler was Mulambwa, the twelfth chief, who ruled from 1812 to 1830. Mulambwa made good laws for the governing of the country, and refused to talk with the Mambari slave traders who came from the Angola coast.

After Mulambwa died the Luyi kingdom was divided, and it was easily conquered by the fighting Kololo who came up from the south in 1838. In the next chapter we shall read about these and other warlike peoples from the south.

# 12 Warrior kingdoms of the south

Let us go back for a moment, and remember that some early Bantu-speaking groups had passed through the Rift Valley, crossed the Zambezi, moved along the edge of the Kalahari, and settled in South Africa.

Some of these groups became the Sotho-speaking tribes, who lived on the tableland between the Drakensberg Mountains and south-west Africa. Others became the Nguni-speaking tribes, or Abenguni, who lived on the southern slopes of the Drakensberg, and in the coastal lowlands. The Sotho and the Abenguni reached the southern part of South Africa between 1600 and 1700.

After 1700, the Abenguni were advancing through Natal. About 1780 they met the Dutch settlers who were moving eastwards from the Cape. A number of wars were fought with these Dutch farmers, who were called Boers, and the Abenguni advance was stopped.

**The Dutch come to South Africa**

Dutch settlers had come to the Cape of Good Hope in 1652. Like the Portuguese, they wanted a place for their ships to find fresh water and fruit on the way to the spice islands of the east. The Portuguese then controlled the east coast of Africa, so the Dutch chose the Cape.

*An old Boer farmhouse*

The climate was so good for white people, that before long the Dutch were establishing farms east of the Cape. They found it was easy to drive out the Stone Age Bushmen and even the Hottentots who had been living there before they came.

About 1780 the Dutch Boers met the first of the Abenguni people, members of the Xhosa tribe, along the Great Fish River. The Xhosa and the Boers fought wars, because they each wanted grazing land for their cattle.

The Abenguni people were now in trouble. Their numbers were increasing, but they could not find new land. The Boers stopped them in the west, and the Sotho blocked them in the north. The Abenguni now began to fight among themselves.

## Shaka and the *mfecane* wars

One of the strongest of the Abenguni tribes was the Mtetwa. Chief of the Mtetwa was Dingiswayo, a great warrior. Dingiswayo trained his soldiers strictly, fed them on beef to make them strong, and armed them with a short broad-bladed spear for stabbing and a thick ox-hide shield. He taught them to fight in a special formation, shaped like the horns of a bull.

The army was divided into regiments according to clans. The leader of one of these regiments was Shaka, of the Zulu clan. *Zulu* means 'people of the sky'.

When Dingiswayo died in 1818, Shaka, with the help of his Zulus, made himself the chief of the Mtetwa. Now the Mtetwa came to be called Zulu. Shaka led the Zulus on conquering raids: north to Swaziland, west into the Drakensberg and south against the Xhosa. The Zulus were undefeated. The terrible Shaka had hundreds of thousands of cattle in his kraals.

The wars which Shaka began spread beyond the Drakensberg as far as the Vaal River. The tribes called these wars the *mfecane*, or the 'crushing'. They were not the work of the Zulus alone, however. Other Abenguni and Sotho groups, driven out by Shaka, set out to travel far away, fighting and destroying as they went.

Let us look at the brief histories of these tribes.

*Late 17th century Dutch painting of the Cape of Good Hope, showing Table Mountain*

**The Kololo conquest of Barotseland**

Some of the Abenguni, led by a Zulu general called Mzilikazi, crossed the mountains and fought the Sotho. Many of the Sotho fled westward. Among them was a band of warriors led by a woman named Mantati. This band or horde, for they were many, prepared to attack the Tswana near Kuruman, but they were routed in a great battle by the Griqua. A small group called Kololo, whose leader was Sebitwane, escaped to the north.

The Kololo spent fifteen years from 1823 to 1838 moving north through the fringes of the Kalahari to the Zambezi. They crossed the Zambezi, defeated the Toka, and moved up to the Barotse plain.

Here the Luyi had quarrelled among themselves since the

death of Mulambwa, so they were easily conquered by the Kololo in four battles. Some of the Luyi, however, escaped north of the Kabompo River. Among them was a boy who was later to become the great chief Lewanika.

The Kololo, under Sebitwane and his son, Sekeletu, ruled Barotseland well until 1865. Then the Luyi, or the Lozi, as they were now called, rebelled and overthrew the Kololo. During that time the people of Barotseland had come to speak the Sotho language and to have many Sotho customs.

**The Ngoni migration**

An important Abenguni group, which broke away from Natal about the same time as the Kololo, were the Ngoni. They were led by Zwangendaba. This great soldier and chief, still a young man, had refused to submit to Shaka's tyranny. He and his ally, Zwide of the Ndwandwe, fought the Zulus but were defeated. Zwide was captured and put to death, but Zwangendaba and about a thousand of his followers escaped.

Although they were few in number, the Ngoni conquered all the people they met on their northward march, and soon had gathered a large and disciplined army.

About 1830 they came to the Rozwi kingdom in Mashonaland. The Ngoni spread fire and slaughter through Mashonaland, burning villages and killing the Rozwi king. They did not stop to settle in the country they had pillaged; instead they crossed the Zambezi near Zumbo in 1835, and marched north. This march took them through Malawi country, up the shore of Lake Malawi. Beyond Lake Malawi, in Ufipa, Zwangendaba died.

Now the Ngoni could not agree who should inherit the chieftainship. The tribe split up, different parts following different leaders.

Mpezeni turned south-west. At once he met the Bemba, and was defeated by them. It was the first great battle that the Ngoni had lost; but you must remember that the tribe had just broken up, and was not as strong as before. So Mpezeni moved south and conquered the Nsenga, before settling in Cewa country south of the Luangwa.

*Zulu chief in full war dress*

*A Zulu kraal*

Mbelwa turned south-east and settled in the hills above Lake Malawi, driving out the Tonga, the Henga and the Malawi tribes.

Gomani took his followers round the north of Lake Malawi and settled north of the Rovuma River, in present-day Tanzania.

**Ngoni language and custom**

You may remember that the Ngoni, when they left Natal under Zwangendaba, had numbered only about one thousand men. Now they had become a great nation or group of tribes conquering and settling in large parts of north-eastern Zambia, Malawi and Tanzania.

This had happened because, when the Ngoni defeated another tribe, they took the younger men captive and trained them to be Ngoni warriors. They also married wives from the subject tribes. These wives became the mothers of Ngoni children. The children learnt the language of their mothers, so that the Ngoni language slowly disappeared. The different Ngoni groups speak the language of the people they conquered— Cewa, Tumbuka, Nsenga, Mang'anga (or Nyanja) and Yao.

Much of Ngoni custom, on the other hand, has lived on. They keep cattle, and the son inherits from the father. They still build their villages in the old Ngoni way. Most important, the Ngoni system of chieftainship has continued.

## Strong chieftainship

When the Ngoni came to southern Tanganyika, they had met those tribes about some of whom we read in Chapter 10—the Nyakyusa, Namwanga, Kimba and Sanga. These people had become used to *Ntemi* chieftainship, which they had learned from the Nyamwezi-Sukuma peoples in the past (see p. 87).

In spite of this, the southern Tanganyika tribes were still small and poorly organized. As a result of the Ngoni conquest, some of these tribes were forced into stronger and larger groups under powerful Ngoni chiefs.

Outside the area of Ngoni conquest, other tribes united in order to resist them. The first of these groupings was that of the Sangu under Chief Merere. His capital was at Utengele in the southern Tanganyika highlands. Next were the Hehe who, under Muyungumba, became strong enough to check Chipeta's Ngoni in the east. In the north, the Nyamwezi continued to be one of the strongest tribes in Tanganyika.

This strengthening of Tanganyika tribes had important

*The migrations of the southern Bantu*

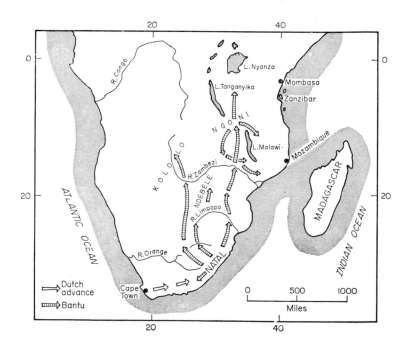

effects when Arab traders came to the region soon afterwards. Some tribes were strong enough to resist the Arabs; others began to make war on weaker tribes, and sell their captives to slave caravans. We shall read about these events in the next chapter.

First of all, however, we must look briefly at one more important tribe which went north from Natal as the result of Shaka's *mfecane* wars.

## The Ndebele

*Lobengula and his wife*

The leader of one of Shaka's armies was Mzilikazi, a great Zulu general. His task was to make war on the Sotho, and terrible battles were fought in the valleys of the Drakensberg.

Now it was Shaka's rule that all cattle taken in war should become his own property. There were huge herds in the royal kraals. After one of his raids, Mzilikazi kept the cattle for his own followers without telling Shaka. The king was enraged and ordered the death of all concerned. Mzilikazi decided not to fight Shaka, but escaped with his army beyond the Drakensberg to the north.

This fighting group came to be known as Ndebele, or Matabele. They made war on the people south and north of the Vaal River, and left charred and smoking villages for hundreds of miles around.

The Boers came north to the Vaal River in 1836. The Ndebele attacked them in two battles, but were defeated by the Boer guns. Mzilikazi then went farther north, to be out of reach of the advancing white men. He crossed the Limpopo and made his capital at Inyati near the Matopo Hills.

From here the Ndebele raided the Shona peoples. They killed them or enslaved them, and took their cattle away. The Rozwi kingdom had been destroyed by the Ngoni ten years before. Now the Shona were finally terrorized and broken up.

The Ndebele also raided the Tswana to the south-west and the Lozi and the Toka across the Zambezi. However, the Ndebele did not try to rule these people or to build an empire. They liked war and plenty of cattle in their kraals.

After Mzilikazi died in 1868, Lobengula became king. There was no change in the Ndebele way of life, and the raids went on as before.

# South-Central African Time Chart

| Date | Southern Africa | Mashonaland | East Coast |
|---|---|---|---|
| A.D. | Sparsely inhabited by Stone Age Bushmen and Hottentots. | Inhabited by Bushmen, with some early Hamites, all of Stone Age culture. | Some Indian traders had long been visiting the east coast. |
| 100 | | | *Periplus of Erythrean Sea* written by Greek trader. |
| 200 | | | |
| 300 | | | Rhapta and other 'Azanian' coastal towns flourishing on Arabian and Indian trade. |
| 400 | | | |
| 500 | | | |
| 600 | | Early Iron Age Bantu settlers probably arriving. | Arab and Persian settlements begin as far south as Kilwa. |
| 700 | | | Decline of Rhapta and other African coast towns. |
| 800 | | Early Karanga (Shona) moving south from Lake Tanganyika. | |
| 900 | First southern Bantu move south of the Limpopo at about this time. | | El Masoudi makes first report of black people living on the east coast. |
| 1000 | | Karanga cross the Zambezi. Karanga kingdom set up between Zambezi and Limpopo. 'Acropolis' building begun at Great Zimbabwe. Arabs visit Mashonaland. Trade begins with Sofala. | Kilwa grows into a large town. |
| 1100 | Early Sotho and Nguni groups cross the Limpopo southward. | | Kilwa gains control of Sofala. |
| 1200 | | | 'Golden Age' of Kilwa begins. |
| 1300 | Sotho and Abenguni slowly move southward, driving out Bushmen. | | |
| 1400 | | Mutota becomes first Monomotapa. Rozwi split away under Changa. Great temple begun at Zimbabwe. Acropolis completed. Portuguese come to Mashonaland. Silveira martyred. Zimba raids. Arab influence returns. Monomatapa drives out Portuguese. Rozwi empire established. Great temple completed. | Kilwa begins to decline. Rise of Pate. Sofala becomes independent. Portuguese arrive on east coast. Kilwa and other towns captured. |
| 1500 | | | Fort Jesus built at Mombasa. |
| 1600 | Sotho established in Botswana and along the Orange River. | | Zimba raiders destroyed. Seif bin Sultan attacks Mombasa, takes Fort Jesus. Portuguese driven from east coast north of Mozambique. |
| 1700 | Abenguni in Natal, now meeting Dutch settlers from the Cape. | | |
| 1800 | Rise of Shaka. *Mfecane* wars. Ngoni, Kololo, Ndebele move north. | Ngoni invasion. Rozwi kingdom destroyed. | Sayyid Said, Sultan of Oman, comes to Zanzibar. Rapid growth of slave trade. |
| 1900 | | | |

## 13 New trade begins in East Africa

For a very long time, traders had come to the east coast of Africa. You may remember that by 600 B.C., and perhaps earlier, traders from the east had been using the monsoon wind for sailing.

Then Arabs and Persians had settled on the coast before A.D. 1000. They built towns which grew into fine cities. After them came the Portuguese in 1498, and from 1500 to 1700 the Portuguese ruled the Arab coastal towns.

*The fortress of San Sebastian, Mozambique*

## Since the Portuguese

We have seen that after 1700 most of the Arab towns were independent again, though the Portuguese still kept Mozambique and the lower Zambezi valley. For over a hundred years the towns went on with their trade as before. Often they fought with one another. Mostly they were under the control of the Sultan of Oman.

Through all this time the trade took place only along the coast. Africans from inland brought their ivory down to the sea. Large expeditions sometimes came from the Nyamwezi kingdom to buy iron and cotton and glass beads from the Swahili and Arabs, and then travel back inland.

People from the coast did not usually go into the interior. In Mashonaland, it is true, Arabs and Portuguese went to live and trade until the Rozwi drove them out in 1693. They were there for the gold. North of the Zambezi this did not happen, because there was little gold, distances were great and parts of the country were dry and forbidding. In northern Tanganyika and Kenya, the Nilo-Hamites, who had arrived about 1600, were unfriendly. They attacked and killed traders who passed through their country.

Because of these things, the people of the coast stayed there. They knew little of the interior. They did not even know about the great lakes, although they believed that at least one lake existed, because the Bantu traders who brought the ivory sometimes talked of the inland waters.

## Beginnings of change

One reason for the decline of the Portuguese had been that other countries were sending ships to the Far East, and taking away the trade of the Portuguese.

These countries were the Netherlands, where the Dutch people live, France and Britain. During the two hundred years between 1600 and 1800, they built up great empires overseas. Britain and France especially became powerful in North America and the Far East.

These countries did not try to make empires in Africa, though they had trading posts on the west coast. This was because they did not think Africa had great wealth. Moreover travel inside Africa was difficult and dangerous, and it was easier to go to other places first.

After about 1750, however, the situation began to change, for two important reasons.

First, because of their empires and growing trade, these countries began to grow richer. In Britain and France especially, machines were invented and factories were built. These could produce many more goods than the old way of working by hand.

People in these countries now wanted to buy more goods from abroad, like cotton to make into cloth, and palm oil for their machines. Such goods are called raw materials. They also wanted more food from abroad, like sugar and spices, to feed the increasing numbers of their population.

Besides buying from abroad, the new industrial countries wanted to be able to sell the things they had made. Their factories produced more goods than people wanted at home, so they needed to find people who would buy them abroad. After a time, traders in these countries came to see that there were many people in Africa who would buy their cloth and iron and other goods.

**Sugar plantations**

The second change was the growing demand for sugar in Europe. Sugar-cane grows in a hot, damp climate. This climate is found in the West Indies. When the people in Britain and France grew wealthier and more in number, traders found that they needed to buy more sugar from the West Indies. They made bigger sugar plantations, and grew more and more sugar-cane.

The people of the West Indies were not numerous enough to do the work. But Europeans do not like manual labour in a hot climate. Traders therefore went to Africa, where people are used to a hot climate. They went to the chiefs and took people away as slaves, paying for them with cloth and other goods. Then they brought these people in ships to the sugar islands, and made them work on the plantations. In this way, as we have read in Chapter 8, the slave trade to the West Indies developed.

After about 1770, people in Europe began to see that slave trading was wrong. Britain stopped trading in slaves after 1807, when a law was passed making such trading illegal. During the next fifty years, the British Government persuaded other European countries to stop it as well. Soon the slave trade on the west coast was ended.

Unfortunately the slave trade in East Africa went on, because the Africans were unable or unwilling to keep the Arabs out, and because Britain could not persuade the Arabs to give it up.

**Arab slave trade**

For a very long time, a few Africans each year had been taken away as slaves from the east coast towns. There were no sugar plantations in Arabia or Persia, but it had always been the custom for rich men to have slaves to be servants in the house and garden.

The number of slaves taken from the east coast in this way had always been small, and they were captured from villages near the coast, not from inland. That is one reason why the Bantu had so little to do with the Swahili. They were afraid of being taken captive, so they kept away from the coast.

Then there were two important developments which made the Arabs want to trade inland. The first of these was the policy of Sayyid Said at Zanzibar. The second was the growing demand for ivory.

*Bateele, or Muscat Arab vessel, used in the slave trade*

*An old elaborate Arab tomb in Zanzibar*

**Sayyid Said**

Since the Portuguese left, there had been quarrels between East African towns. Zanzibar had grown more wealthy and important. Mombasa with its great fort was always a strong town. The Sultan of Oman found it difficult to control the East African coast.

In 1804, Sayyid Said became Sultan of Oman. He was a strong, ambitious man. He wanted to be master of the whole Indian Ocean trade. Zanzibar was loyal to him, but he soon found that Mombasa was not. With its proud rulers of the Mazrui family, Mombasa was determined to be independent. In 1823 the Mazrui even tried to win British support, but they gave up when they found that the British were against the slave trade.

After many attempts, Sayyid Said at last forced Mombasa to submit in 1837. Three years later he left his home in Oman, and came to live in Zanzibar. He knew that he had to do this if he was to control the east coast towns and Indian Ocean trade.

**Clove plantations**

Now Sayyid Said resolved to make Zanzibar as rich as possible through trade. There was the ivory trade already, but ivory came from inland, and not from Zanzibar itself. Sayyid Said thought that cloves would grow well in Zanzibar.

*Clove plantation and cloves*

Ivory

Cloves are a sweet-smelling spice much liked by people in Europe. The Sultan started some clove plantations after 1840, and encouraged others to do the same in Zanzibar and Pemba Island. In a few years there were many clove plantations.

Now cloves have to be harvested twice a year, and much labour is needed to cultivate them. As a result the Arab planters soon began to send expeditions into the interior of East Africa to buy slaves.

Before long the number of slaves being collected in East African towns was greatly increased. Most of them were brought to the markets at Kilwa, Zanzibar and Pemba Island. The slaves who could not be sold for plantation work were put on ships and taken to Arabia and Persia.

The second reason why the Arabs on the coast wanted to trade more inland was that people in other countries needed more ivory.

The population in Europe was increasing, and many people

were growing richer. They were able to buy more goods made of ivory. Ivory was used in making parts of musical instruments, especially piano keys. It was also used for brush handles and billiard balls and furniture decoration. Ivory therefore became more valuable. Sayyid Said and other Arabs started to bring more and more ivory from the interior. As the trade of Zanzibar increased, some Arabs became very rich. More Indians, whom the Swahili called 'Banyans', came to settle in Zanzibar. They acted as bankers and lent money to Arabs who wanted to start plantations or send out trading expeditions.

These expeditions went farther and farther into the interior, sometimes for hundreds of miles.

**Trade routes**

The earliest trade routes used by the Arabs were from Pangani and Bagamoyo opposite Zanzibar and Pemba Island.

The route from Pangani went two hundred miles north-west to Chaga and south Masai country, near Kilimanjaro. Here there was much game and there were great herds of elephant.

In 1850 an expedition of a thousand men set out from Pangani. There were the Arab leaders riding on donkeys. There were many bearers, Swahili and Bantu, carrying food for the journey and goods to trade with. These goods were mostly cloth and ironware and glass beads, and were worth about £4,000. Then came armed soldiers, carrying guns and spears, to protect the travellers from attack. Some tribes, like the Masai, did not like traders, and tried to stop them passing through their country.

After some months inland, the expedition came back to Pangani with many elephant tusks, some rhinoceros horn, and some bags of hippopotamus teeth.

Sometimes it was possible to send two expeditions in the same year. An average of 35,000 lb. of ivory passed through Pangani every year.

The second early trade route used by Arabs went west from Bagamoyo. This route was long and difficult. It passed through dry country where travellers became hot and thirsty. Then, after reaching the Upper Rufiji River, it went through Ugogo to Unyanyembe, about five hundred miles from the coast.

Unyanyembe, which was near modern Tabora, was in the heart of Nyamwezi country. The Nyamwezi were a strong tribe, and were able to bring slaves as well as ivory to the Arab

*Zanzibar from the sea: an early
19th century sketch*

traders. It became a big trading centre. The journey from the
coast took many weeks, and it was not easy to return the same
season. The Arabs made a settlement at Unyanyembe. Some
Arabs made their homes there, and did not return to the coast.

**Farther inland**

In their search for ivory, the Arabs went even beyond Unyanyembe.

First, they travelled northward, round the south and west
shores of Lake Nyanza. This was the lake region. Here the
Ganda people had broken up the Nyoro Empire and became
the strongest kingdom. Arab traders first came to the Ganda
capital in 1843.

Next, the Arabs travelled from Unyanyembe to Lake Tanganyika. On the shore of the lake, in south Burundi, they made
a settlement at Ujiji. After 1851, they crossed the lake on boats
and went into Congo country, capturing slaves. They even
reached the Lualaba, which is the Upper Congo River.

Third, the Arabs found their way round the south of Lake
Tanganyika, to Lunda country on the Luapula. They made a
settlement at Kazembe's village. Here there was a great deal
of ivory, and also copper from the Katanga west of the Luapula.

These were the main Arab trade routes. They were mostly covered by expeditions from Zanzibar.

**Other routes**

There was one other important trade route. This went from Kilwa, south-west across the Rovuma River, to the south end of Lake Malawi. Arabs crossed the lake in boats to Kota Kota. From there, some went across north-eastern Zambia to Kazembe's. In Nyasa country, again, the trade was mainly for ivory and slaves. After 1860, the Yao became a slave-raiding tribe, and sold their captives to the Arabs. The Portuguese also sent some slaves down to Mozambique.

Another Arab trade route went from Bagamoyo to the north end of Lake Malawi. There Arabs made a settlement, in Ngonde country. Some travelled from there, north of Lubemba, to the Luapula.

You can see these routes on the map on p. 118. They were mostly made by Arab traders between 1840 and 1860.

*A carved doorway in Zanzibar*

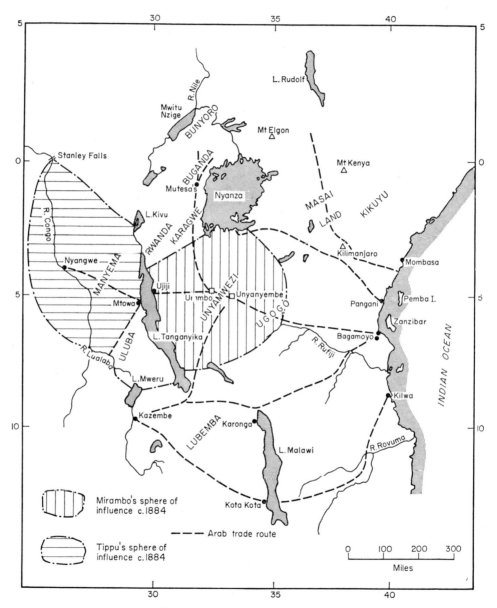

*Arab trade routes about 1840–1884*

Map labels:
L. Rudolf
Mwitu Nzige
R. Nile
Mt Elgon
Mt Kenya
BUNYORO
BUGANDA
Stanley Falls
Mutesa's
Nyanza
MASAI LAND
KIKUYU
L. Kivu
R. Congo
RWANDA
KARAGWE
Kilimanjaro
Mombasa
Nyangwe
MANYEMA
Ujiji
Urambo
Unyanyembe
UNYAMWEZI
UGOGO
Pemba I.
Mtowa
Pangani
Zanzibar
L. Tanganyika
Bagamoyo
R. Lualaba
ULUBA
R. Rufiji
L. Mweru
INDIAN OCEAN
Kazembe
Karonga
Kilwa
LUBEMBA
L. Malawi
R. Rovuma
Kota Kota

Legend:
Mirambo's sphere of influence c.1884
Tippu's sphere of influence c.1884
— Arab trade route

Scale: 0 100 200 300 Miles

# 14 Arab traders move inland

We have seen that Arabs found their way into the interior of Africa between 1840 and 1860. This happened firstly because of the growth of world trade and secondly because of the policy of Sayyid Said. These Arabs were few in number, in a very big country. But they were powerful because their followers carried guns, and because the tribes needed the goods which the Arabs brought to sell.

We have also seen that when the Arab traders went a great distance inland, they were too far from the coast to return each year. For this reason they founded trading settlements, and stayed to live. Such settlements were at Kazembe's on the Luapula, at Karonga on Lake Malawi, at Ujiji on Lake Tanganyika, and at Mutesa's in Buganda. The largest settlement was at Unyanyembe in Nyamwezi country.

**Trading chiefs**

After a time, the Arabs at some of these places made themselves into chiefs, with authority over the clans and villages far around. Then they would control the ivory and the slave trade in that area. They did this because they wanted to grow wealthy, not because they were interested in the people of the country. They planned that, when they were old, they would retire to the comfort of the coastal town. There they would be able to buy a big house, and settle down with many servants.

At least one African chief followed the example of the Arabs and built up trading empires based on the sale of ivory and slaves.

The people in the villages obeyed the trading chiefs because they were not strong enough to resist, and because they wanted protection from the slave-raiding tribes that began to trouble the country.

As the slave trade grew, there was more war and fighting. In Malawi and Tanganyika, the Ngoni invasion had broken up many small tribes. The Ngoni themselves had split up into parts. Groups of warriors now wandered about, attacking villages. They were called *ruga ruga*. They served any master who would pay them well. They attacked villages, plundered them, and sold slaves to the Arabs.

In Malawi the Yao raided the smaller tribes for slaves. In

(left)
*Tippu Tip*
(right)
*An early photograph of
ivory carriers*

north-eastern Zambia the Bemba did the same. The Yao and
the Bemba sold the slaves to the Arabs.

Because of all this trouble, the smaller tribes preferred to live
under a trading chief, even if he was an Arab. They might not
like the Arab, but at least he would protect them from the
*ruga ruga*. Let us look at the two greatest of these trader chiefs.

Tippu

Tippu Tip was an Arab who made an empire in the Congo
highlands west of Lake Tanganyika. His real name was
Muhammad bin Hamid. He was born in Zanzibar, and grew
up to be a trader on the Unyanyembe route.

When Tippu came to Unyanyembe in 1850, he saw that to
obtain more ivory it was necessary to rule the tribes. In this
way he could be sure that ivory from every elephant killed
would be brought to him and to no one else. There were already
several Arabs in Unyanyembe, so Tippu crossed Lake Tanganyika and made an empire in the Congo highlands. Here, great
herds of elephant roamed the country.

The people of Uluba lived simpler lives than the tribes to the
east of Lake Tanganyika, and Tippu easily subdued them. He

fought the Bemba south of the lake, and defeated them as well. Then he went north, down the Congo as far as the Stanley Falls, and said that these lands were to be kept for the trade of the Sultan of Zanzibar.

Tippu ruled all this country as overlord from 1860 to 1884. Twice he came back to Zanzibar with huge expeditions carrying ivory. One expedition carried about two thousand tusks.

In 1885 the Europeans meeting in Berlin said that the Congo basin should be controlled by King Leopold of the Belgians. The Arabs felt that they could not fight the Europeans, so Tippu went back to Zanzibar.

**Mirambo**

While this was happening west of Lake Tanganyika, another trading empire was built up east of the lake. In Unyamwezi, the Arabs had their settlement at Unyanyembe. At first, the Nyamwezi people were friendly to the Arabs. Then, after 1850, trade increased. The Nyamwezi decided that they should share in the gain from this trade, and Chief Manua Sera tried to make the Arabs pay tax. The Arabs refused, and there was fighting between them.

In 1865 Mirambo became a Nyamwezi chief. He was not

*The Stanley Falls and rapids on the River Congo*

*An illustration of 1861 showing a slave chain-gang in Central Africa*

the chief of the whole Nyamwezi people, but he was a strong character and became the most powerful chief in the country. He made his capital at Urambo, about fifty miles from Unyanyembe.

Trade began to go to Urambo instead of Unyanyembe, and Mirambo became stronger than the Arabs. He built forts called *bomas*, with great mud walls, in different parts of his country. *Ruga ruga* came to fight for him, and he extended his rule to Ujiji on Lake Tanganyika, and as far as Ugogo in the east.

Mirambo's empire lasted until his death in 1883. Two years later, German ships came to Zanzibar, and forced the Sultan to agree that the trade of the interior as far as Lake Tanganyika should belong to Germany.

**Sultan Barghash**

Let us see what was happening on the coast in the time of Tippu and Mirambo.

The great Sayyid Said had died in 1865. He was succeeded, first by Sultan Majid, and then in 1870 by Sultan Barghash. Barghash was not as ambitious as Sayyid Said, but he was a good and wise ruler.

Barghash became a friend of the British consul at Zanzibar, Sir John Kirk. Kirk said that the slave trade was bad and ought to be stopped. He said that if it were not stopped, the British Government would send ships to prevent Zanzibar from trading with anyone. Barghash agreed to do as Kirk asked. He made laws stopping the shipment of slaves from Zanzibar, and closed the Zanzibar slave market.

This made it more difficult for traders from inland to sell their slaves, so the slave trade gradually grew less. At the same time the ivory trade began to decrease because so many elephants had been destroyed.

Finally in 1885, as we have seen, the German Government forced the Sultan to give them the trade of the interior. After this, the Arabs made one more attempt to have a trading empire. It did not last for long.

**Mlozi**

Because of German activity, some of the Arabs decided to move south, and open up a new slave and ivory trade between Lake

*Arab slave convoy: an artist's impression*

Malawi and the Luapula. Slaves and ivory from here were brought to Kilwa, and sent away in ships.

The most important 'Arab' taking part in this trade was Mlozi. He was not really Arab, but Swahili. Mlozi made his settlement near Karonga in Lungonde, at the north end of Lake Malawi. Many slaves were sent to Kilwa from Ngonde, Henga, Tumbuka, Mambwe and Tabwa country. Some were even sent from Kazembe's lands on the Luapula.

In 1887 the missionaries at the north end of Lake Malawi tried to drive out Mlozi, but they were not strong enough. They tried to teach the people to grow crops so that they could buy their cloth from the Europeans instead of from the Arabs. But this takes a long time, and there was too much fighting to allow the people to settle down and learn.

In 1891, however, Nyasaland became part of a British Protectorate, and at last in 1895 the British Commissioner, Harry Johnston, arrived with troops. He defeated Mlozi and put him to death. A few Arabs escaped to the Luapula, but soon they too submitted to the British.

*A British warship destroying a slave dhow on the east coast of Africa: a mid-19th century drawing*

## The Arabs in Buganda

In the north, the people of the lake region were too strong for the Arabs to make an empire. Arab traders lived at the Kabaka's capital, but they were guests and paid respect to the Ganda king.

Because the Arabs were in their country, the Ganda people became wealthy and powerful. They took all the Arab trade, and prevented it from going to the kingdoms of Butoro and Bunyoro. They were able to do this because, after passing through Karagwe, Buganda is the first country which traders come to from Unyanyembe.

The Arab trader Muley bin Salim taught the religion of Islam to the Ganda, and by 1875 Kabaka Mutesa was a Moslem. He took on some of the Moslem customs, copied some of the manners of the Sultan of whom he had heard, and lived in greater state than before.

## Changes brought by the Arabs inland

We have seen how the Arabs lived and traded in the interior from 1840 to 1890. This is quite a short time, but important changes in the life of the people happened as a result.

First, the slave trade increased greatly. By 1860, twenty thousand slaves a year were sold in the Zanzibar market. There were also smaller markets in the other towns.

Second, the slave trading led to more wars between tribes. Tippu and Mirambo kept peace and order in the centre of their countries. But outside these countries, tribes fought one another in order to take prisoners captive, and sell them to the Arabs for cloth and guns. Many villages were burned and people killed in this way.

Third, many more guns came into the country. Some tribes gave up fighting with spears, and used guns instead. They also used guns for hunting. Elephant and other game began to disappear in parts of the country.

Lastly, more cloth and other goods came into the interior. The custom of making bark cloth began to die out, and so did other customs and crafts which villagers had pursued in more peaceful days.

## Arab influence declines

As we have seen, the Arabs were driven out when the Europeans came to control this part of Africa.

European interest in Africa had been growing since the end of the eighteenth century. This interest had been awakened by the journeys of James Bruce in Ethiopia (1768–71) and of Mungo Park along the Niger (1796 and 1805). With the coming of the factory system and new methods of transport, people in Europe saw the possibilities of developing other continents and of bringing Christianity and education to their peoples. Africa, a huge continent, lay close to them, but they knew little about it. By 1860, however, brave travellers had made their way into the interior: René Caillé, Richard Lander and Heinrich Barth across the Sahara to the Niger; Richard Burton and John Speke from the east coast to the source of the Nile; David Livingstone from the Atlantic to the Indian Ocean by way of the Zambezi.

*The Peace Museum, built on the site of the old Zanzibar slave market*

Using quinine and other medicines to protect themselves from tropical disease, other travellers and traders followed.

The early travellers and traders in East Africa, and the missionaries who came with them, saw that the slave trade was cruel and wrong. They remembered how the similar trade to the West Indies had recently been stopped, and asked their governments to end the fighting and slaving in East Africa as well.

The European governments, especially that of Great Britain, were anxious to end the slave trade, but were unwilling to spend the necessary money. However, they saw that proper trade might help to pay for the cost of administration. Above all, business men wanted to be able to import minerals and raw materials, and to be able to sell goods made in their factories to the people of Africa as well as of other continents.

For these reasons, when European control of East and Central Africa began after 1880, slave trading and Arab influence in the interior quickly disappeared. Of course, although the slave markets were closed, Arab and Swahili traders continued living in the east coast towns, where they are important even to this day.

# 15 West Africa and the Fulani

In the last six chapters we have been reading about developments in East Africa, both on the coast and inland, roughly during the four centuries from 1450 to 1850.

We shall now cross the continent again to West Africa to see what was happening there. First, look back to Chapters 4 and 8. These chapters will remind you of two important events that had affected West Africa in the fifteenth and sixteenth centuries. The first was the coming of European traders to the coast. The growth of the slave trade and of foreign influence helped to change the balance of power among the coastal kingdoms. It also slowed their development. The second event was the Moroccan conquest of Songhai after the battle of Tondibi in 1591. This destroyed the civilization of the Niger empires, and broke up western Sudan into small kingdoms.

Thus by the eighteenth century West Africa consisted of many separate states, often trading, but sometimes warring, with one another. The great systems of Mali and Songhai had long disappeared. Even the powerful city states of Oyo and Benin had become corrupt and lost their influence. In the Niger cities, learning and Moslem worship had declined.

**Revival begins**

At the end of the eighteenth century, however, new efforts began to create new states and to revive religion and learning. These efforts were made in the Sudan region, north of the forest belt, in areas where the effects of the slave trade had hardly reached.

Here, on the Upper Niger, were the old city states of Segu, Timbuktu and Djenne. Farther east, the Hausa towns continued to trade between the desert and the south, and often to fight with one another. At this time the strongest among them were first Zamfara and then Gobir. To the east again lay Bornu and the dusty villages of Kanem.

All these states had long been Moslem in name, but good Moslem teachers had become few. Pilgrimages to Mecca were rare, and rulers had given up strict Moslem laws and made use of pagan custom. A great religion, however, cannot die away easily, for there are always efforts to renew it. This happened in West Africa.

**The Fulani**

This Moslem revival started among the Fulani of Hausaland. These nomadic cattle-herdsmen were Hamitic or Berber in type, rather than Negro. Their original home was far to the west, around the headwaters of the Senegal River, in the country called Tekrur. Once subjects of the kingdom of Old Ghana, they had for centuries been wandering eastward, leaving settlements all along the Niger. Since 1450 they had become numerous in Hausaland and Bornu. Some lived in the towns, but most of them remained herdsmen in the countryside.

Many Fulani had become Moslem. The country Fulani, however, kept a purer faith than the townsmen who, as we have seen, had increasingly mixed with the Negro inhabitants and turned back to local custom. One particularly strong Moslem group were the Toronkawa, a Fulani tribe with some Arab blood.

*Fulani villagers*

**Usuman dan Fodio**

To this Toronkawa branch of the Fulani belonged Usuman dan Fodio, leader of the greatest religious revival in West Africa since the Almoravids. Claiming descent from an early Fulani chief in Senegal, Usuman was born in Gobir in 1754. Well taught by his father and uncles, he became a devout Moslem. When he was only twenty years old he began preaching tours in Hausa towns, where he soon won many followers.

For thirty years Usuman continued teaching and preaching, mainly in Gobir. He published booklets in Arabic and poems in the Hausa language. Many people listened to him and read his books.

Naturally Usuman found himself increasingly in trouble with the authorities in Gobir. In 1788 the Sultan of Gobir plotted his death, but Usuman had too many supporters, and instead the Sultan had to grant him freedom to preach whenever he wanted. Ten years later the new Sultan Nafata made another attempt to stop the new movement by forbidding conversions to Islam, and also by banning the wearing of turbans, which was customary among Usuman's followers.

In spite of these efforts, the new movement grew steadily year by year. At last in 1803 Nafata's son, Yunfa, a former pupil of Usuman's who had changed his mind when he became Sultan, decided that his position would not be secure as long as Usuman lived. He planned to kidnap Usuman at Degel and have him killed.

**The *jihad* begins**

Usuman was warned of the plot, and on 21 February 1804, he escaped to Gudu just in time. His followers called this escape the *Hijra*, thus comparing it with the Prophet Mohammed's escape from Mecca in 622.

Usuman, now known as the Shehu, decided that the time had come to wage a holy war, or *jihad*, against the unbelievers of Gobir. His message was simple. In Hausaland there were many pagans. Furthermore, many who were Moslems in name had given up the true faith. True Moslems should withdraw from the society of these unbelievers and pretenders and join the *jihad* against them. Gobir especially, he argued, was an infidel state because its ruler had shown himself to be no longer a Moslem and because of the superstitious practices followed there.

Within a few months the Shehu had raised a large force

from followers who flocked to join him. In June 1804 his army defeated the Sultan of Gobir at the battle of Tabkin Kwotto.

As a result of this victory, many new supporters, mostly Fulani, joined the Shehu's army. They looked far beyond Gobir. The *jihad* was turning from a local religious campaign into a war of conquest. Usuman himself did not take much part in the fighting; a great scholar rather than a soldier, he wrote pamphlets and booklets for the guidance of his followers. His brother, Abdullah, and his son, Mohammed Bello, took command of the armies. After four years of fighting they captured Gobir and killed the Sultan in October 1808.

By this time most of Hausaland was controlled by the Shehu. In the following year, 1809, he made a new capital for his growing empire at Sokoto.

### The *jihad* in Bornu

To the east of Hausaland lay Bornu. Here some of the Shehu's enemies had taken refuge. The Shehu therefore made war on Bornu and conquered it. The last of the Sefawa kings was turned off his throne, bringing the thousand-year-old dynasty to an end.

However, east of Bornu again lay the old kingdom of Kanem, whose ruler, El Kanemi, was a learned man and a devout Moslem. El Kanemi denied that the people of Bornu were pagans, or that they had become pagans by harbouring the enemies of Usuman. They were true believers, and the Shehu had been quite wrong to make war on them.

El Kanemi therefore raised an army himself, and finally drove Mohammed Bello out of Bornu in 1810. Consequently Bornu and Kanem remained outside the Fulani Empire.

### The Fulani Empire

Most of Hausaland, however, was now ruled by the Fulani followers of the Shehu. Usuman himself died in 1817, but the administration was carried on by Mohammed Bello, who became Sultan of Sokoto and controlled the northern part from Zamfara to Kano, and by Abdullah, whose capital was at Gwandu and who looked after the southern area around Nupe and Ilorin.

While the empire was being built up, each expedition commander had been given a flag of authority by the Shehu. These commanders were therefore known as flag-bearers. As each province was conquered, the flag-bearer was appointed as emir

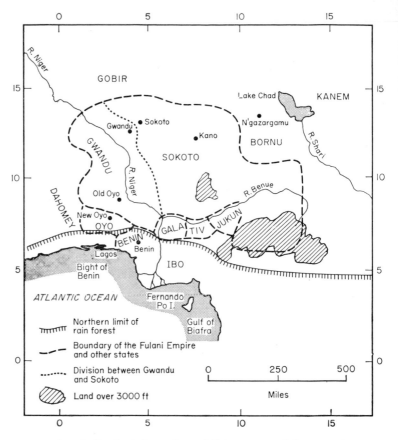

*The Fulani Empire about 1830*

to run the civil administration. All but one of these emirs were Fulani.

The emirs ruled according to principles laid down by the Shehu, who himself had made a careful study of Moslem law. These principles covered such things as the working of the law courts, the collection of taxes, the control of the treasury and the administration of markets.

As time went on, the authority of the Sultans of Sokoto and Gwandu grew less, until each Fulani emirate became virtually independent, though continuing to pay tribute. The Fulani leaders intermarried with the local Hausa populations of the towns. None the less the Fulani Empire continued to exist until the British gained control of Hausaland at the end of the century. Its law and administration have continued to influence the government of Northern Nigeria down to the present day.

**The Five Rules of Government**

... and I say—and help is with God—the foundations of government are five things: the first is that authority shall not be given to one who seeks it. The second is the necessity for consultation. The third is the abandoning of harshness. The fourth is justice. The fifth is good works.

And as for its ministers, they are four. The first is a trustworthy wazir to wake the ruler if he sleeps, to make him see if he is blind, and to remind him if he forgets; and the greatest misfortune for the government and the subjects is that they should be denied honest wazirs. And among the conditions pertaining to the wazir is that he should be steadfast in compassion to the people, and merciful towards them. The second of the ministers of government is a judge whom the blame of a blamer cannot overtake concerning the affairs of God. The third is a chief of police who shall obtain justice for the weak from the strong. The fourth is a tax-collector who shall discharge his duties and not oppress the subjects.

*Usuman dan Fodio*

# 16 Influences on Africa's history

We have now read about the story of Africa and its peoples as far as about 1850. Many books recount the events that happened after that, as the result of trading and colonizing competition among the European powers. The aim of this short chapter is not to go further forward with the story, but to look back and to sum up the situation at that time.

To begin with, let us consider what have been the greatest forces influencing Africa's development during the past two thousand years. We can pick out seven main ones.

**The foundations**

First, there is the land itself. A massive continent, Africa has two notable characteristics. One is its isolation. Although close to, and in fact linked with, Europe and Asia, its interior is difficult to approach, partly because of the desert barrier in the north and partly because its rivers are not navigable very far. The second characteristic is that Africa lies across the equator. This gives much of it a decidedly tropical climate. The effects of this climate on human development have been described in this book. It has also meant that the same conditions are to be found in the north and south of the continent. The peoples of Africa have been able to move from one part to another and find familiar grasslands, forests, deserts or mountains. This has perhaps encouraged the migrations that are a feature of Africa's history.

This brings us to the second big influence on the history of Africa: its peoples. We have seen that these are a blend of aboriginal types with Negroes and Hamites, and with some Semitic and European elements as well. The largest groups are the Negroes and their cousins, the Bantu-speaking peoples, and to these we usually apply the word 'African': they are the chief inhabitants of tropical Africa. Truly, however, all inhabitants of the continent could be called African. They are varied and vigorous peoples, with great cultures of their own, all of whom have played a part in the important story of human development that belongs to the African continent.

Thirdly, there is the influence of Ancient Egypt. One of the earliest and greatest civilizations in the world, the Egyptian civilization lasted for three thousand years. That is twice as long as European civilization, which has grown out of the ruins of the Roman Empire. It happened on the African continent, and its peoples were Africans of one kind or another. Though separated from tropical Africa by the desert belt, the influence of Egyptian belief and custom, passing through Meroe, has been felt in different ways all through the continent ever since. Some of these ways have been described in this book.

**Religion**

The fourth great influence has been the religion of Islam. This influence has of course been greatest in North Africa and in the Western Sudan from the Upper Nile to the Upper Niger. Here it has formed the faith of millions of people, and made possible study and learning. Sometimes it has caused religious wars. It has also helped to create large states like the Songhai Empire, in which people have been able to live together in peace and order. The east coast of Africa also has been marked by the civilizing influence of Islam; but here the Arab and Persian settlers usually put trade before religion. Islam did not spread inland until about a hundred years ago, when Christian missionaries were also at work.

This fifth great influence, Christianity, did not affect most of Africa until after the period covered by this book. Christianity in North Africa declined after the Romans left, except in Egypt, and finally disappeared when the Moslems came. The Christian church of Aksum, later Abyssinia, remained cut off in the Ethiopian highlands until recent times. Portuguese attempts to convert Africans after 1500 in West Africa, Angola and Mashonaland met with little success and were spoilt by trading ambitions, and especially by the slave trade. Christianity did not really begin to come to most of Africa until the European explorers showed the way for the missionaries in the nineteenth century. At that time medical discoveries were also making it possible for Europeans to live in a tropical climate.

Two of the great things the Christian church then did were first to insist on the slave trade being stopped, and second to help the African peoples through the difficult seventy years of colonial rule, especially with education. However, those achievements lie outside the scope of this book, which has told the story of Africa before the partition began.

**Other foreign influences**  The sixth influence has been foreign trade. In spite of its isolation for reasons which we have seen, there has been some trade between Africa and the rest of the world for thousands of years. It has always been the possibilities of trade which have drawn foreign peoples into Africa. Even across the Sahara this trade has taken place, helping to create the wealth which built the empires of the Niger. The rest of Africa, of course, could only be reached by using ships. The Indian Ocean trade along the east coast, as we have seen, was a very old one. It was not till the Europeans learnt to sail far out on the oceans after 1400 that the great trading peoples of Portugal, Holland, France and England began to reach Africa. Their trade grew, at first slowly, and then after 1850 very quickly. Slaves were only a part of this trade though, for a time, a large part. By 1850 slave trading by European countries had been stopped, and had been replaced entirely by the exchange of manufactured goods for raw materials.

None the less it is a fact of Africa's history that trade, which should have been a useful and civilizing influence, often did more harm than good at the beginning. Too often it promoted war or disturbance, and helped to break up growing African states like Oyo and Benin in the west, Mbanza Kongo in the centre, and Monomotapa's empire in the south-east. More recently the harm done to the Congo region by the oil and rubber trade in the time of the Congo Free State is well known. Perhaps this was because much early trade was not real trade, but involved the use of force and deception.

One of the great difficulties about trade in Africa has of course always been the absence of proper transport and communications. Only since they have been provided in this century has Africa really begun to benefit from trade.

This brings us to the seventh and final influence, which has been the period of colonial rule. This began in most parts of Africa after 1875, and ended in most parts after 1960. You can read about this in other books. The many effects of this period are obvious to anyone living in Africa, from political boundaries and ways of government and official languages to roads and mines and railways. Here we shall just say three things about it.

First, it was probably inevitable, because European countries which experienced the industrial revolution were growing rich and powerful so quickly compared with other parts of the world.

Some good as well as bad effects resulted. These bad effects probably ought to have been prevented, but the colonial period as a whole was bound to come.

Second, it is unlikely that Africa could have caught up with the modern world in any other way. Even now Africa is still catching up. The old, really African cultures are still growing together with modern ways of life. This growing together will continue for a long time. It is a good process. It is only from the mixing together of different influences that new good ideas can come. This will happen in Africa.

In the last century it was not so easy to see this. To conclude, we shall turn back once more to look at the condition of Africa a hundred years ago.

## Africa a hundred years ago

When foreign travellers made their way into the continent during the last century, they found a great deal of disorder. If you look through the time charts in this book, you will see that this was so, and perhaps why it was so. In the western Sudan the Negro states, as a result of the Fulani *jihads*, were only just beginning to recover from the effects of the Moroccan invasion three hundred years before. In the forest belt of the west coast, wars caused by slave trading continued to make settled life difficult, while Oyo and Benin had grown feeble and corrupt. The same conditions affected the Congo region. In East Africa the appearance of Arab traders inland brought slave trading and war, and the spread of guns and powder. All south-east Africa was also disturbed by the effects of the *mfecane* wars in Natal. These had been partly caused by the conflict between the southern Bantu and the Boers. They resulted in warrior tribes like Ndebele and Ngoni migrating north and bringing war to the lands north of the Limpopo.

All this encouraged foreign visitors to describe Africa as a barbaric land of war and disorder. Many books gave this description. However, we can see that it was not altogether true, because not all Africa was disturbed like this. More important, Africa's past was far from being always a period of disorder. To a large extent it was foreign invasion and the wrong kinds of foreign trade during the previous three centuries which had helped to make these conditions prevail.

Anyone who reads thoughtfully about Africa's past will see that history is not one long story of upward progress. It is a story of stops and starts, of going forward and then backward before going forward again. One thing which is certain is that Africa today is at the beginning of the greatest stride forward in all her history so far.

# North African Time Chart

| Date | West Africa | North Africa | Ethiopia |
|---|---|---|---|
| B.C. 500 400 | Early Berber trade across the Sahara. | Phoenicians settling on North African coast. | More Hamites from Arabia settling in Ethiopia. |
| 300 200 | Iron Age reaches Nok community on Jos Plateau. | Rise of Carthage begins. Conquest of Carthage by Rome in the Punic Wars. Roman rule in N. Africa begins. | |
| 100 A.D. | | Roman rule completed by conquest of Egypt. | Growth of Aksum with port at Adulis as centre of trade between Upper Nile and Red Sea. |
| 100 | Small Mandingo chiefdoms on the Upper Niger River. | | |
| 200 300 | | Greatest extent of Roman Empire. | Aksum now capital of great kingdom. King Ezana destroys Meroe. First obelisks set up. Christianity accepted in Aksum. |
| 400 500 600 | Berber kings begin to rule in Ghana. | End of Roman Empire in west. Vandals overrun N. Africa. Destruction of towns like Leptis. Berber tribes alone survive. Camel reaching Sahara. | Great age of Aksum. |
| | | **THE *HIJRA* 622** | |
| 700 | Za kings begin to rule in Gao. | Arabs conquer Egypt. Arabs conquer the Mahgrib, cross to Spain. Abbasids overthrow Umayyads, found new capital at Baghdad. | Aksum cut off by Mohammedan conquests. 'Dark Age' of Aksum begins. |
| 800 900 | Soninke (Negro) kings establish rule in Ghana. Visit of El Fazari. | Beginning of Fatimid Empire in N. Africa. Cairo founded. | Appeal from King of Aksum to King of Nubia goes unanswered. |
| 1000 1100 1200 | Kingdom of Ghana at greatest extent. Almoravid conquest. Islam begins in Ghana. Collapse of Almoravid rule. | Beginning of Almoravid Empire. Ghana conquered. Almohads replace Almoravids in the Mahgrib. Mahgrib breaks up into separate states. | Zagwe line of kings set up. Rock-hewn churches built. Centre of kingdom moves south to Amhara. Last Zagwe king overthrown. Solomonic line restored. |
| 1300 | Sundiata founds Empire of Mali. Growth of Islam along Niger. Musa's *hadj* to Mecca. Mali Empire at greatest extent. | | |
| 1400 1500 | Sonni Ali founds Empire of Songhai. | | Conquests of King Zara Yakob. New Moslem invasion. Appeal to Portuguese for help. Moslems driven from Abyssinia. Isolation of Abyssinia continues. |
| 1600 | Askia I conquers Mali (1590). Greatest extent of Songhai-Moroccan wars. End of Songhai Empire. | Moroccans overthrow Songhai at Tondibi (1591). Moroccans withdraw to north of desert. | |
| 1700 1800 | Fulani Empire begins. | | |

# Questions and exercises

These questions are included for general guidance. Teachers will of course have other exercises and questions of their own. In particular, pupils should be encouraged to illustrate their notebooks with maps and drawings taken from the text.

**Chapter 1**

1 Explain why Al Mahgrib became separated from the rest of the Arab Empire.
2 Write a paragraph about Ibn Yasin and why he was important.
3 What influence did the Almoravids have on West Africa?

**Chapter 2**

1 Explain the importance of gold, slaves and salt to the trade of Ghana.
2 What developments took place in Ghana under the Soninke kings?
3 What were the effects of the Almoravid conquest upon Ghana?

**Chapter 3**

1 Write a short life of Sundiata.
2 Imagine that you accompanied Mansa Musa on his pilgrimage to Mecca. Describe your experiences.
3 Write down four things reported by Ibn Batuta about the Empire of Mali.

**Chapter 4**

1 Who were (a) the Songhai and (b) the Za Kings?
2 Compare the character and achievements of Sonni Ali and Askia the Great.
3 Explain the importance of the battle of Tondibi.

**Chapter 5**

1 Explain how Bornu became an important kingdom in 1500.
2 Do you think that the legend of Abuyazidu is a satisfactory account of the beginning of the Hausa Bokwoi? Give reasons.
3 How did the Hausa manage to keep their independence?

**Chapter 6**

1 Imagine that you are a brass craftsman in Ife about 1300. Describe your work and trade.
2 Why did the Alafin of Oyo become such a powerful ruler?
3 Explain why the Yoruba Empire finally broke up in the eighteenth century.

| Chapter 7 | 1 | What was the influence of the Portuguese on the kingdom of the Kongo? |
|---|---|---|
| | 2 | Describe the achievements of Shyama Ngoongo among the Kuba. |
| | 3 | Three peoples are described in this chapter—the Kongo, the Kuba and the Luba. Write down two things which interest you about each. |

| Chapter 8 | 1 | Describe the part played by Henry the Navigator in the Portuguese exploration of West Africa. |
|---|---|---|
| | 2 | Why did the European traders fight against one another more than against the African inhabitants of the west coast? |
| | 3 | Why did the Africans not only fail to stop the slave trade, but even take part in it themselves? |

| Chapter 9 | 1 | Why did the Portuguese first come to East Africa, and why did they seize the Arab towns? |
|---|---|---|
| | 2 | What difficulties did the Portuguese meet with in Mashonaland in the sixteenth and seventeenth centuries? |
| | 3 | Why did the Portuguese finally give up most of the East African towns? |

| Chapter 10 | 1 | Who were the Chwezi? What benefits did they bring to the lake region? What happened to them after the Lwo invasion? Draw a plan of the Bigo earthworks. |
|---|---|---|
| | 2 | Who were the Lwo? Why did they invade the lake region? Make a list of the kingdoms set up by the Lwo. |
| | 3 | Who were the Nilo-Hamites? Write a paragraph about their character and beliefs. Why did they think they had a right to other people's cattle? Find out where they live today. |
| | 4 | Explain why the Ganda became a powerful tribe. |
| | 5 | Why did the Kikuyu not learn to have chiefs until recent times? |

| Chapter 11 | 1 | Why are some of the Malawi called Mang'anja, while others have different names? |
|---|---|---|
| | 2 | Describe the part played by Chitimukulu I in the history of the Bemba tribe. |
| | 3 | What is meant by the 'Lunda dispersal'? |

| Chapter 12 | 1 | Explain the reasons for the *mfecane* wars. |
| | 2 | Describe the effects of the Ngoni migration on countries north of the Zambezi. |
| | 3 | How did the Ndebele come to live north of the Limpopo River? |

| Chapter 13 | 1 | Explain why the Arabs started slave trading in the interior of East Africa after 1800. |
| | 2 | Draw a map of Arab trade routes into the interior. Through what African tribes did they pass? |

| Chapter 14 | 1 | Who were the *ruga ruga*? (See also Chapter 12.) How did they affect developments in East Africa? |
| | 2 | Describe the part played by either Tippu or Mirambo in the development of East African trade. |
| | 3 | What were the effects of Arab trade in the East African interior? |

| Chapter 15 | 1 | Who were the Fulani? |
| | 2 | Write an account of the life of Usuman dan Fodio in three paragraphs. |
| | 3 | What was the importance of the Fulani Empire for that part of West Africa? |

| Chapter 16 | 1 | Make a list of the seven main influences on the history of Africa. Can you think of any others? |
| | 2 | Why did many foreign travellers look upon Africa as a land of barbarism and disorder a hundred years ago? |
| | 3 | What do you think were the three most important effects on Africa of the period of colonial rule (not described in this book)? |
| | 4 | If you were writing a history of Africa a hundred years from now, what topics would you include for a chapter on the 1960's? |

# Index